SUBURBAN WILDERNESS

SUBURBAN WILDERNESS

William Jon Watkins

G. P. *Putnam's Sons*
New York

Library of Congress Cataloging in Publication Data

Watkins, William Jon.
  Suburban wilderness.

  1. Animals, Legends and stories of. I. Title.
QL791.W28   1981   818'5402   80-19164
ISBN-399-12552-3

PRINTED IN THE UNITED STATES OF AMERICA

For Sandra,

Yesterday I saw
a cardinal in the buff,
and two
(redder than scarlet)
in a fir tree
against the hands of green;
the gray styling of a mocking! bird,
the white crescents of its flight;
Outlaw biker starlings
Groucho Marxing on the snow,
foot-after-foot, like a man
walking on stilts
with lizard feet attached,
for laughs;
a stickpin sparrow
on a fingerthin branch;
two mourning doves
in Victorian morning clothes;
the blue jay
planting oak trees
in the mulch of the rain gutter

and you!

And for Tara, Wade, and Chad, the rest of the
species.

SUBURBAN WILDERNESS

The Mad Squirrel

The Mad Squirrel was an omen, a sharp break in the flow of ordinary events that illuminates all events that follow and makes whoever sees it reinterpret all events that have gone before. He lived in a locust tree beside my garage for a year and a half while the rest of the Squirrel nation lived in high rises of oak and sweet gum in the vacant lot across the street.

He was not mad most of that time, but he looked it. His tail was almost defoliated, a pine tree blasted by invisible storms. He was a derelict, I believe, or at least an outcast marked by some vision greater than the imaginings of his peers.

He was the toughest of a tough lot, and I wondered sometimes if he had not been sent into exile like some Roman nobleman for the good of the Republic. If he had been a banished Greek, hot for his brother's throne, he could certainly have gone back and taken it by force. It was not as if the vacant lot across the street was more of a journey than he could make. I saw him come and go across the dog-watched, cat-spied street a hundred times; he never crossed the same way twice.

Sometimes he would take the cover of the hedge along the Ryans' house all the way to the far edge of the sidewalk, alternately scrambling and lying spread-eagle-flat in the grass. Other times he'd wait until the shadow of the house stretched as far as it would go toward the street, crouching in it a half-step from its edge, doing head twists like a fighter who knows he's loose. Other times he took the hedge in darting leaps, a rookie running back with a foot in each row of invisible tires.

But no matter what personal ritual he went through to get himself psyched, once he left the curb, he came straight on across toward the network of trees and roofs that meant safety. The last sane crossing he ever made came on a dead run, down the biggest sweet gum in the middle of the lot, over the mine field of spiky gumballs, and straight across the macadam in five-foot leaps. I don't know what he was running from or to, but he almost didn't make it.

Halfway across, he had to turn sharper than a UFO, spinning on a hind leg that seemed to have become suddenly stuck to the ground, to swerve away from the tires of a passing car. He looked like a midget leading a bull the size of a house in a *passé Verónica*. I half-expected him to turn that Buick around and run it by under his armpit again just to get another *olé*.

But he didn't. He just crouched there, all four of his feet rooted to that macadam, his sharp, black hooks curved into crevices in the stone. Even the brave get shaky when their skill pulls them out of the jaws of death by reflex. He looked as if the strongest wind in memory was still roaring in his ears. His eyes bugged out, and his whole body swelled up and shrank with each heartbeat. He stood there throbbing, like a man who has just heard his death whistle by like a too-close train, and realizes that it has not, *Thank God!* stopped . . . this time.

The two Siamese cats and the Black Dog stopped what they were doing and snapped up their heads as if some silent scream had gone out on the wind. I wondered if the squirrel would make it, and I had an impulse to go out on the porch and chase away any of the predators that happened along, but I had made a promise that, like an alien species, I would not interfere with the daily life of the natives.

So I watched him through the window, while he panted, a third of the way across the street, in full view, frozen by the closeness of death. Through the binoculars, I could see deep in his eye a floating reflection of himself fighting its way to control through the syrupy fear. I could see the cats moving from the south end of the block, crossing and recrossing the street to avoid the Black Dog, who strained at the end of his chain. The squirrel could see the two Siamese, too: Carrunner and Wise Teacher.

Carrunner understood exactly where the Mad Squirrel was weak. He had been to that frozen moment himself, drowning in the adrenalin crisis, and he had acquired an unquenchable taste for it. He had gotten so good at the angle of pursuit that took him into the orbit of death that he could touch his whiskers to the hum of the tire and put his nose right up against the burned rubber of the brakes. He was running like à legend then, and he could recognize the first blossom of mortality craziness in the squirrel.

Carrunner came down the far side of the street with that cocky strut he only put on when he knew he had a one-winged bird flopping in hopeless panic in the leaves. He knew exactly how long it would take the squirrel to come out of that ecstatic paralysis, and he had the chase calculated down to a microsecond. I could tell from the drift of his walk that he planned to maneuver Wise Teacher out of the way and catch the little rodent when he made his last leap for the tree on the far side of the flatway.

Wise Teacher moved more sedately. He had his own estimates, and he was quite willing to let Carrunner make his bid for the prey. The Blue Point had a fast streak, but he had bad hooks, and the prey often got away even after he had surrounded it. Wise Teacher had Seal-Point reserve. He had already taken the situation into consideration and had chosen the conservative route. Over the long haul, prudence would carry his life past the Blue's by half a decade if he had a little luck.

There was no point in racing Carrunner; Wise Teacher would lose three times out of five. I had seen him test it. Once Wise Teacher had established the Blue's speed, he laid back and let Carrunner do the running. To lose three times out of five was an energy drain that led to short life. As long as the Blue missed half of the prey he caught up with, Wise Teacher was content to wait and snag the easy meal just outside the zone of capture. But if push came to shove, he was not above reaching in and taking the mouse out of the fence of arms the Blue put around it.

But the Blue was young, and if he didn't get himself killed playing on the flatway with the rushing of death, Wise Teacher would have to do something about him someday. Meanwhile he took the easy living and waited.

Wise Teacher had been to the frozen moment only once, but he knew it in more detail than the Blue who ran his whiskers against it with increasing madness. He knew its progress like the nightmare that comes curled on the forbidden cushions in an empty house. He knew the adrenalin daze, had risen himself foot by foot to the surface of action.

He knew from a long, quiet watching of the Blue that if a creature liked that paralyzed rapture, it was addictive. Probably he saw the first tracks of adrenalin junkiedom in the squirrel's eyes, as well. In any case, the odds were three to two that the Blue would miss the squirrel even if he caught up with it. The odds were even that Wise Teacher would get it on the rebound. They doubled in his favor the more swipes of the hand he got a chance to make. He had hooks faster than the eye, come by the hard way—through hours of practice in the sun, trying to beat the dark shape of his shadow.

The dark companion was a puzzle of infinite concern to him. He never seemed to quite figure out the stretching, shrinking shape that mocked his own. The distortion of his darker nature moved when he moved, threatened when he threatened. If it had gone only that far, he could have learned to ignore it, but it struck when he struck, passing away into his own strike, catching his best move, or stretching out of shape to avoid it; dragging back along his arm, mocking him.

He had gotten good by working against that phantom, and if the Blue missed, the chances were nine to one Wise Teacher would hook it if he got a second shot. The first shot is always the prey's best chance in close. There are only two ways out, and flight is always first. The squirrel had a full circle of escape routes. Only when all of them were closed off would he fight to tear himself free. Carrunner recalled only the bizarre familiarity of it. Wise Teacher remembered the flash it had put into his muscles, leaping him away from the teeth of death three times as far as he knew he could go, so fast it didn't even leave a memory except a bright flare of pure terror. He knew how strong those legs were growing on the panting squirrel.

If Carrunner ran it down, the odds were good that Wise Teacher would get the meal. He could erase the circle of attack in front of him in three scimitar-shaped swipes. If the creature was still in the original strike zone when Wise Teacher finished his rolling strike, it would be down and bloody. But the odds were not nearly so much in their favor

that the Blue would make a capture. Terror could carry the
squirrel out of their grasp like a ghost.

The cats walked slowly for a reason. Fresh out of his
trance, the squirrel could go by even Carrunner on the
rush of his fear. The longer they waited, the lower the
blood flickered, and the easier the capture. There was an
art to it, which Wise Teacher had been trying to teach
Carrunner for a year, subtly, without word or admonition.
When Wise Teacher went slowly to conserve energy for the
final rush, Carrunner could not dart ahead without looking
like a foolish kitten about to get its nose tweaked, and he
knew it. Every time he got two body lengths in front of
Wise Teacher, he slowed down. The last time Carrunner
had run ahead of an elder, he had come whisker to teeth
with the Black Dog, who haunted his dreams and drove
him toward the wheels.

The further ahead he got, the more daunted he became.
Whenever he got four lengths ahead, he stopped and let
Wise Teacher catch up with him. It was a small compulsion but it allowed Wise Teacher to maneuver him into the
best position from which to make a run.

I had watched Wise Teacher over and over, working
Carrunner up and down the block, trying to teach him
patience. He sharpened Carrunner's perceptions without a
word, beating him time after time, until Carrunner
watched his slightest move, looking for the clue that would
let him know Wise Teacher was going to force him to
attack by attacking first. It was a matter of life and death
for Carrunner, even in the long run. A student is kept for
the prey he brings into the master's sphere. He was a
student, an apprentice aristocrat being taught the ways of
his kind and class. A mixed breed or an untrained Siamese
hunted with the body, a purebred like Wise Teacher
hunted with the mind. Without training, Carrunner was
only a half-step ahead of the crossbreeds, and age would
eventually put him half a step behind them. Without Wise

Teacher, he was just another fast runner streaking toward an early death. With half the tricks Wise Teacher had, he would still be able to make it when his legs went and he started coming out of his crouch like a winter housecat getting up from a warm spot near the radiator. It was a symbiosis only an aristocrat would understand.

It was a gentleman's agreement; Wise Teacher would provide instruction in return for the larger portion of everything caught above and beyond what Carrunner had caught before. The price of instruction diminished as the apprentice learned more and could command a greater share of the catch. Learning to kill on the run had given Carrunner the chance to make his own uninstructed kills, on which he was entitled to as much as he could ravage before Wise Teacher claimed his share, taking the choicest parts and leaving just enough to keep Carrunner fit and ready to hunt. Still, Carrunner got his money's worth. Wise Teacher had taught him to make his running strike three moves ahead of the victim's first escape. The path varied with the prey, and he had had to learn the pattern, watching Wise Teacher time after time until he could tell where the darting bodies would come together, yards in advance of where they ran. Slowly he was learning where a mouse zigs and when it zags, until he could take it three patterns into the run.

He could not yet read the signature of the prey in its first movement the way Wise Teacher could, but he could project a pattern like a wavering line in front of anything running in front of him. Gradually he would be able to decide where he would take the prey, sauntering down the street, long before it had any knowledge that he was there. When he was his own Wise Teacher, when he could take all the prey and give nothing, he would have graduated. He could take his own apprentice then, or choose to stay as a full partner.

Wise Teacher could move himself into the outer orbit of

a prey's awareness so that his quarry had nowhere to run but the route of Wise Teacher's intention. When he had learned that, Carrunner would force the confrontation and win his freedom. If he tried too soon, he would get put in his place with a lesson of claws and sharp cuffs.

Still, every move he made was a move toward his freedom, and there was a limit to how long he could wait. If Wise Teacher held him off long enough, he would find himself passing his prime before he learned to so shape the motions of his attack that there could be only one result, precisely and exactly what he intended. From Wise Teacher he would learn to shape his actions so that days in advance, the precise spot and method of the kill became inevitable. In the reality of cats, Wise Teacher was making him into a shaman—a wiseman/crazyman/medicineman/poet. Even the wheels were part of his training.

Wise Teacher moved him into position. The odds were dropping toward even. The squirrel was fighting out of his rapture before they were finished. It was a ticklish situation. There was a haze between the slow, predictable flight of the adrenalin doldrums and the unguessable craziness of the adrenalin rush. Taken an instant too soon, the squirrel would leap out of its terror in a way that could not be predicted. Taken at just the right instant, on the far side of its haze, it would run with smothering slowness into inevitable capture. Timing made all the difference.

Taken in the first valley after the initial spike, the prey was almost helpless. It was an empiric subtlety Carrunner had yet to grasp, and he frightened the prey into action too soon more often than not. Eight lengths away, Wise Teacher had to decide whether to make a bid for the kill. There were risks either way. If he had to use something new to make the kill, Carrunner was that much closer to equality and his freedom. If he made the bid and missed, he could always pretend to pass it off as a test of

Carrunner's alertness. But there was still the chance of loss of face.

A test was unavoidable from time to time, to see where they both stood. Wise teachers who lost their apprentices almost always failed to test them often enough, but every test exposed another of the master's techniques until he put himself into a corner where he had to use his best to take the prey. Once Carrunner was sure he had learned Wise Teacher's last trick, he would try to go it one better and win his freedom. It was expected, and Wise Teacher would eventually have to drive him off if he did not have the initiative to strive for his mastership. To do otherwise was to defraud the customer.

Carrunner paced slowly in front of him, staring at the prey, trying to fix the method of its flight in his mind. He knew it was a bounder, quicker than it was fast, more elusive in the sharpness of its turns than a mouse or a rat. The chemicals of his brain fed him messages that flashed a warning spike of adrenalin. Hooks! It had hooks and could make a deep wound if taken wrong.

He could feel the rhythm of fear in his blood, an anticipation that meant it was a kill that had to be made from behind, on the run. Carrunner had learned the precise point in the tiny bobbing ball of fur where the tip of his claw should go in and catch to rip the creature forward over itself and break its neck.

Carrunner went two more body lengths before he began to get nervous. When he looked back, Wise Teacher was not there. He was moving off at an angle a couple of body lengths away. Carrunner began to do the same, trying to keep exactly to Wise Teacher's pace, keeping his mind focused on the prey. Wise Teacher kept his eye on the prey at all times, watched it from a block away so that it moved inescapably into the swipe of his paw in a continuous series of actions, each of which arose from the one before it.

By the time they were opposite each other with the squirrel between them, Carrunner could see the intention. Wise Teacher would cut it off from the advantage of its home territory and force it back onto less familiar ground, where it might make a mistake, and Carrunner's swiftness could overtake it. A moment's hesitation between leaps, any break in the continuous motion of its flight, and Carrunner would make a capture.

But Wise Teacher had another motive. The squirrel had a full circle of options; it was full of its fear and faster than the dark, elusive shape whose smothering attack he could never defeat. The odds were against Carrunner making a capture, but they were against Carrunner being turned on and raked as well. It was a safe test for the student—little danger, a wide variety of opportunities for mistakes. If the capture failed, Carrunner would have to watch Wise Teacher make the maneuver again and again before he could see where he had made his error. Where there was grave danger to his apprentice, Wise Teacher would make the kill himself or soften up the prey before allowing Carrunner his chance.

Otherwise, unless the situation was a new one or had some undetermined inconsistency, he let his apprentice take the risks. If he brought his follower along slowly but strictly, Carrunner would develop into an excellent hunting partner at best and a worthy slave at worst. The problem lay in which way to train him. The energy drain of hunting for two until two could hunt like three was very steep, and the rapid method made an apprentice capable of bringing in a second full portion of prey much more quickly. The quicker method paid back the deficit of time and energy from reduced catches sooner, but Wise Teacher had long-range plans for Carrunner.

Bringing an apprentice along slowly led to a hunting partnership that could carry a wise teacher as far into old age sometimes as a natural death. The survival of the species favored it; the former apprentice would eventually take an apprentice of his own and begin the process all over again. Wise teachers were better fed and lasted longer; they had their choice of mates and could spread the advantages of their learning more quickly within the genetic mix. Wise teachers conserved their energy, wasting the energies of their amorous competition, their apprentices, in the hunt. The balance shifted always in favor of the best knowledge, the most valuable transmission for the species. Privileges of rank were the price the species paid for learning.

Everything Wise Teacher did centered around the poles of gathering information and conserving energy. His wisdom came from maintaining a constantly updated picture of everything that went on in his territory. His advantage was the power of information, but the information did not come easily. It came from walking interminable rounds, exploring the unusual, the disordered, at every turn. Even a mystery that had been marked by some itinerant dog had to be reinvestigated and logged in detail. Curiosity feeds the cat; it only kills those who fail to weigh the risks against the opportunity correctly. Experience by experience, Carrunner was learning the basic premise of cathood: opportunity comes from places that have changed in some way since the last round.

Chance is the great giver, the god of catkind. Carrunner and Wise Teacher were followers of chance where it could best be seen—in change. In following changes in their territory, they followed the rewards of chance encounters. The out-of-place sound of screeching brakes had drawn them like a dinner bell. Food can be anywhere for the astute.

Wise Teacher kept such a detailed vision of his world intact that he could tell at a glance what had been there while he was gone. All creatures disturbed the territory in a pattern that identified them to him. How they moved, what they smelled or tasted, where the disturbance was spread, and how things had been handled told him what had been there and why. Patterns of disturbances led to food; Wise Teacher had enlightened curiosity.

He had a passion for conserving energy, as well. The movement of a cat who is stalking is more efficient than the walk of one who is strutting for approval or out of pride. Carrunner strutted continually. Wise Teacher moved as if he was riding up and down waves of energy, sliding along them rather than walking. He seemed to ride everywhere. When he ran, he was a blur of feet, skimming along a wire of efficiency and immediate feedback that could end nowhere but in the prey. He glided toward the squirrel the unusual noise had shaken out of nowhere into their laps.

The squirrel's eyes seemed almost full of consciousness, but his body was still panting. Wise Teacher went after him slowly. The squirrel could be fully awake, waiting for a clear opening or an unguarded moment. If he was taking that great a risk, he would have to be either desperate and thereby dangerous, or a tough customer as likely to go on the offensive as retreat. Wise Teacher tested the alternatives cautiously. The squirrel was still panting as Carrunner closed in on him from behind, but Wise Teacher was still careful. The squirrel might be stunned or even grazed, but there was only one way to find out. He approached close enough to swat at it.

The sharp points of Wise Teacher's hooks swung within half an inch before the squirrel twisted and flung himself in the opposite direction, his claws outstretched. He was a pinwheel of little scimitars whirling into Carrunner's face. Even Wise Teacher would have flinched out of the way.

The squirrel went over Carrunner's shoulder on the fly and landed in a heap behind him. He came rolling out of his fall on the dead run. Carrunner made a halfhearted swipe at the path of the squirrel's escape and uncurled himself after it with a mortified howl. He would have had the squirrel in two bounds, but it sprang onto the wispy ropes of forsythia hedge beside the Ryans'. Tan as bamboo, thin as fingers, the hedge was a precarious escape. Unless the squirrel could make a leap to something higher before he got too far up, he would sink back in a long parabola into waiting death.

The squirrel went up like a gymnast up a rope, using his feet like an extra set of hands. Two thirds of the way up, he became like a pole-vaulter, falling down the bend of his fiberglass pole and dipping back toward Carrunner. Curled for a leap when the squirrel reached his lowest point, the Blue waited with learned patience.

But the squirrel swung around the trunk and whipped it aside as he leapt for a thicker hedge spire and scrambled up it. Two leaps later, he rode the dip of the top fork of hedge up onto the lowest runway of the sweet-gum tree. Two bounds and he was on limbs thicker than his hind legs, high enough for the cats to look his own size again. Distance diminishes fright, and he sat in the fork of a sound, round limb chittering about the narrowness of his escape. I could see in his eyes, mixed with the receding fear, a longing for that moment of imminent danger that he could not resist.

He looked as if he had just had a strong euphoric and wanted another, but he calmed himself by peeling an imaginary nut. By the time he had finished his rosary, he was already mapping his route home, calm, collected, reasonable; an entity that knows its own niche. But I knew by his eyes that he was hooked.

Once, in the depth of my own adrenalin addiction, I had a motorcycle that I would ride at the top of its speed until the front wheel wobbled and shook me like a fist in the face of my mortality. I knew the junkie thrill of careening toward the dark edge, and I knew he would follow that addiction to its brutal end.

From the moment the wheels missed him, he had ceased

to be truly a squirrel. Squirrels of both sexes are prissy old maids. They are prudent as burghers; solid, land-holding gentry, full of petty rituals and folk wisdom. They keep up a constant chatter about the safety of the woodlot that is half public service, half gossip. Their strong point is conservative measures, efficient routines, attention to detail. Squirrels are tough customers who avoid fighting whenever they can. They have survived by learning to fly without wings because they prefer the risks of free fall to combat. Trapped, they are the kings of infighting who make cats look like amateurs, but they are not noted for bravado or heroic recklessness. They are the yeomen of the woodlot; sturdy, belligerent, righteous, patriotic.

Squirrels are not prone to heroic fatal gestures. They court death on the ground with steady uneasiness. The ground is an exhilarating place to visit, but it is not a place a sane squirrel would want to live. A sane squirrel is always uneasy going from nut to nut, seed to seed. His real advantage is in the branches, in the faith that allows him the blind leap into empty space.

On the ground, he is just another fleeing target looking for a vertical handhold. Almost everything that isn't vegetarian will eat a squirrel, and a dog will kill one for practice. Bravura in a squirrel is so unheard of as to be an omen. An omen is a spectacle of nature, a display of events and actions that is so striking that it cannot be interpreted in any real way except as a microcosm of the flow of things, the shadow of something ineffable passing through the workings of the world. The rise and fall of the Mad Squirrel was an omen.

I watched him every day as he went crazy. I believe he became so afraid in that moment when his reflexes pulled him from under the wheels of the car that he had to keep putting himself in danger to prove that he could not simply be swept off the planet at any instant. The roar of his death had come so close that he could only stop hearing it by going closer and closer to the real thing.

His madness was small at first and barely showed for almost three days. He went home with no more than three short runs on open ground. He darted from tree to car to flatway and up a rope of branch from the roof of my car. It probably made a difference that he went on the ground at all, something like getting back up on a bike a year after a bad accident. Only madmen get back up on a disaster without sufficient cause.

He waited in the tree for a while, worrying about twilight when the cats' eyes would bring them into their element, and watching Wise Teacher give Carrunner lessons in close quarter self-defense. Half an hour went by before Wise Teacher lifted his head from tracing hypnotic designs on the ground under the tree and spotted the Orange Cat watching his secret teachings from the far end of the lot like a spy satellite.

His pursuit was immediate, and he was almost to the far street before Carrunner caught up with him. The Mad Squirrel came scurrying down the tree and along his escape route. A more prudent squirrel would have spent the night away from home in a not totally unfamiliar tree and chanced an early morning return. A clever squirrel would have watched the pattern of the cats' visits to the lot and passed over the street once they had gone past on their rounds.

But this squirrel had become a brave squirrel, a throwback to some savageness squirrels had left behind in the infancy of their culture. It was an act of madness.

It was only the beginning. By the third day, he was hanging down from the slender tips of locust vine scolding the Little Dog with the Big Voice. On the fourth, he was dropping to the ground in plain view and scurrying around in frantic figure eights. He was completely mad by the time he began dropping off low hanging branches beside dogs out on leashes.

There is a locust tree in front of the house with straggly, downturned branches that hang down to head level, and two pines with branches across the sidewalk low enough to have to duck under. The squirrel began to hang like a Christmas-tree ornament on one of the lower branches, and when a dog came through on a leash, he would drop down beside it out of nowhere and give it a running scold before darting up the next tree. Before long, he was dropping out of the first tree and running just beyond the dog's teeth all the way to the third tree in the line.

Sometimes when he dropped alongside a trotting dog, he would turn and look right into its eyes, daring it to break stride and take a bite out of him. He got crazier by the day. Pretty soon it didn't matter whether the dogs were leashed or not. He dropped down and taunted all of them. He would look them right in the teeth and dance away scot-free.

But even that wasn't dangerous enough for him after a while. I could see that adrenalin decay set in, like something running too fast too long. He got so he had a junkie look in his eye, like the only time he was alive in the whole cycle of the day was those few instants when he danced right up against his death and danced away again without a scratch.

If he wasn't flushed with adrenalin, he was falling apart. His rituals became twitches. He would sit in the tree, dropping down a series of branches and climbing back up to do it over again like some cliff diver practicing for the finals. He would perch on a high branch and dive straight down without a handhold or a breakfall for a dozen body lengths. When he came to a branch, he hooked it and yanked himself past it like he was climbing up a ladder instead of falling like a dropped nut toward the center of the earth.

Every lurch downward was an act of faith, but mere falling was not enough. He began to drop on dog owners, running down their arms or their backs. Once he ran down a man's arm and more than halfway along the leash before the dog choked itself backward trying to get him off. He had men and dogs going down in heaps. He had women screaming profanities. He even drove the cats crazy.

Every time Wise Teacher and Carrunner went by under his trees, engrossed in their silent intelligence gathering, he would be sitting in the highest tip of the tree, swaying like a lookout in the wind. He was beating the cats at their own game. He could follow them down the street, knowing that every action they would make under the tree was fixed by the way they had come down the street. He knew more about them than they did about him, and it made him as good as invisible.

He could outsmart Wise Teacher because he had better information and he had it sooner. He watched the cats come, learning what made them keep their heads down, what made them look to one side or the other. By the time they passed under his tree, he knew exactly which series of branches to come hurtling down to drop near their flanks and give them a slash. Other squirrels fluttered in the tree lot like birds, scolding him to give up his flamboyant ways and regain his senses.

But there was no limit to his madness. He began dropping on the cats in places they were sure were safe, halfway around the block, and darting away again before they could recover. It made them look foolish even in their own eyes, and they began to avoid the block. Dogs started barking at the corner whether he was in the tree or not, and their owners started going on up the avenue instead of turning down the street. It was inevitable that he went on the offensive.

He went to the lot to do it where he had plenty of room. He started three bounds and a final rising leap from the oak tree. As soon as he left the ground, he twirled himself in a pinwheel and caught the thick ridges of bark with his claws. Anchored that way, he slashed downward in a surprise counterattack. It took him dozens of tries before he could catch the bark every time coming out of that spinning, twisting leap, and he practiced it dozens of times after that.

When he had gotten it to a reflex, he baited the Black Dog. The Black Dog stalked the dreams of every creature in the woodlot. When his leash pulled loose, terror spread like fire through the neighborhood. The Mad Squirrel waited until he came, dragging his master at the end of a chain. He lay flat, his tail stretched out behind, downwind from the sidewalk, still as a twig until the Black Dog jerked past. Then he sprang up chittering, his tail bristling, his eyes popping with exhilaration. The dog startled. The squirrel held his ground. Held it longer. He held until I was sure he had frozen again. The dog dove toward him; the chain stretched, snapped. I thought the squirrel was dead meat. But he whirled aside and bounded for the tree. He was only six inches ahead of the teeth when he got there.

He misjudged the height of the dog's jump, and instead of reaching down, he found himself slashing the side of the dog's head as it went by. The dog's shoulder hit him and he flew off the tree. I thought he was finished. But he hit a perfect distance from the trunk and waited for the dog to come roaring around the tree. When it did, he led it through a figure eight and whirled into his defense.

He hit two feet higher on the tree and in perfect position. His downswipe ripped into the dog's nose and his hooks went through halfway around their curves. The howl of the dog tore them free, and the squirrel flew tumbling twenty feet out from the tree like a ball thrown out of a jai-alai scoop. He hit on his head and flopped over like he was dead.

The dog could have had him for torment, but he was sneezing blood and pawing at his face as if he had been disfigured and disgraced. His tail had dropped between his legs as if he knew what the incident was going to cost him in status on every fence post and tree. He would have to do deference or fight any dog who lolled a tongue at him. The thought of some clever wag imitating the scent his pain was spreading across the lot hurt him more than his nose. The thought of the Little Dog with the Big Voice mimicking him on every mailbox and curbstone was a nightmare. The squirrel lay stunned, but the dog tucked his tail further between his legs and ran off.

The squirrel had destroyed the Black Dog in a very real sense, but it did him no good. He seemed to go into a decline after that, as if he had no more worlds to conquer. It was inevitable that he would have a confrontation with the Blue Jay. There is a natural antipathy between the upstart leapers and the true fliers that would probably have erupted even if the jay hadn't provoked it. A squirrel spends a lot of time in free fall, but it is not, after all, a bird! It may have been that fact that gnawed at the squirrel. It may have been that the raucous, disdainful scolding of the jay reminded him that no matter how ferocious his bravery, he would always be no more than a squirrel. Probably the jay himself had no choice in the matter; he was crazy by profession.

The Blue Jay acted toward the rest of the woodlot like a thug landlord, attacking and threatening everybody he saw. He was a belligerent, noisy braggart and a bully like the rest of his species. Everyone respected and despised him. He was the warden of the woodlot, with a crankiness that was directed at everything that moved. He lived under a constant stress that bordered on paranoia. It made him as crazy in his way as the Mad Squirrel.

Every intruder was a personal affront. The jay seemed to believe that everything he could fly over was his, and he spent most of his day trying to chase every interloper from the face of the earth. Every jay is an angry owner who thinks everyone else is a trespasser. A blue jay doesn't take a backward step from anything, not even human beings. Armored in righteous indignation, the jay protects the sanctity of property.

But no property is as sacred as the preserve around the nesting tree. An intruder there will call down on himself an unremitting attack until he is driven off. The Blue Jay was no respecter of size. Nobody intimidated him. He rapped on the heads of dogs, poked his sticker in the ears of cats, and pinched God's nose in his beak. It was tantamount to suicide when the Mad Squirrel went up to take the sweet-gum bristles from under the jay's favorite tree. It was the worst sort of challenge, short of climbing up into the nest.

The jay dive-bombed him off the premises with bloody raps to the head and painful pecks at his shoulders. He forced the squirrel back away from the tree and kept hammering at him until he got under cover of the hedge, where the jay would have had to land to get at him. Then he cruised the woodlot doing barrel rolls and cursing all unwinged things.

The jay had left him sore and bloody, and any other squirrel would have made a note to pay closer attention to territorial boundaries and chalked up the bruises to experience. But the Mad Squirrel was no ordinary squirrel, and may not, by that time, have been a squirrel at all. I saw him the next day, curling himself into a ball and whirling up off the ground like the good guy in a karate movie.

I believe the jay must have seen him as well from his sailing perch up near the glass roof of the woodlot, because when the Mad Squirrel went back under the nesting tree, the jay scolded and threatened but he stayed up in his branch. The squirrel didn't come up the tree either, and it seemed a smoldering standoff. They fought a war of attrition after that, with the squirrel trespassing further and further up the lower trunk of the nesting tree, and the jay taking a clear shot at the squirrel whenever he got a chance. He was good at sneak shots, dive-bombing out of nowhere. The squirrel used it against him eventually.

The squirrel hadn't had a genuine adrenalin fix since the Black Dog, and it began to take its toll on him. He began to move with a crazy jerkiness, like a constant twitch. It was an affront to the jay. He tolerated squatters until he could drive them out, but he would not tolerate a weakling. A jay-ruled woodlot is a tough town. When the squirrel began acting erratic, it drew the jay like a thumbed nose and he dove in from behind.

He did not realize it was a trap until it hit him. Just before he slowed to stall speed to peck, the squirrel rolled forward. The jay hovered; the squirrel snapped himself into the flying-swords move he had perfected and buried his hooks in the feather armor of the jay's chest. Two hooks went in clean and came out leaving little red dots on the white feathers. They had to go a long way in before they struck anything, and they curved too soon unless the hand was cocked precisely. But the hooks that caught were torn out again with the twirling fall of the squirrel. He whipped the jay past him, and it looked for an instant like the jay was going to nose-dive into the ground.

But the jay did a long, twisting roll the length of the tree and slid up off the ground like he was on a string. The squirrel had had his best shot; the jay had been lucky to escape. If the Mad Squirrel had let it stop there, he might have come to no grief. But he couldn't.

Squirrels have a determination that makes them so hardy, but it can degenerate into stubbornness. When a squirrel loses his sense of self-preservation, when he becomes entranced with touching death as it goes by, the way the Mad Squirrel had, that stubbornness turns deadly.

The Blue Jay refused combat thereafter, but the squirrel's madness would not let him rest. He came every day to the bottom of the jay's tree and chattered what had to have been squirrel obscenities, but the jay ignored him like an aging heavyweight champ ignoring a challenger he beat by a split decision. The squirrel waited until the jay went up to survey his domain from the top of the world and the mother jay had fluttered down for a caterpillar. Then he shot along a trail of branch runs and falling leaps that carried him down into the Blue Jay's nest.

If the master jay had not been intentionally ignoring him for so long, he might have swooped down in time. But his pose delayed his counterattack just long enough for him to lose everything. Eggs and nest were shredded in an instant. The mother jay shrieked toward the Mad Squirrel, but he had left her nothing but revenge.

She dive-bombed him in the shreds of the nest and drew blood between his ears with a rock-hard rap of her beak. The squirrel braced a foot partway up the thickest branch. She swung back in on a branchlet above his head. It was sticky with yolk where the squirrel had raked an egg up and out of the nest. The instant her feet wrapped around the branch, the horror of what the stickiness was seemed to hit her and she froze.

It was perfect for the squirrel, and he threw himself up at her in his whirling attack. His hooks tore at her chest plate of feathers, but he drew only a little blood. His other hand hooked her shoulder, the curving points going in through the webbing near the forward arch. The female jay shrieked, the male cursed and dove. The squirrel twisted his hooks like a dockworker. The male jay landed on his back, digging his spurs into the fur. The squirrel let the female go and shifted his feet to pull the true object of his raid off his back. It left an opening he could not cover; the jay reared back and stuck his foil into the squirrel's eye and plucked it out like the seed out of a fallen fruit.

The jay's peck dropped the squirrel through the tree like a stone. He hooked a backhand and a trailing foot often enough to break his fall, but he hit bottom going backward and lay like a crumpled rag at the foot of the tree. If the mother jay had left him there, there would have been an end to it. But she had nothing left, and an eye was less than payment for the agony of a brood patch with no eggs to soothe its maddening itch. For nothing to feed when her own appetite disappeared in the overwhelming urge to hunt food, an eye was no payment at all. She dove screeching for the squirrel. It was a fatal mistake.

The torn wing wasn't strong enough to pull her up and she struck next to the Mad Squirrel with an impact that cracked her wing backward like a broken gate. She fluttered clear of the squirrel, but her wing was too damaged to fly. She seemed to have hurt her foot in the landing, and she flopped and hobbled in a wide circle, trying to get under the cover of the hedge. If she snuggled in among the leaves and lay motionless, the cats might go by her.

The Blue Jay swooped down in front of her and when the cats came, he fought a desperate, bloody fight to keep them off her. But in the end, Wise Teacher held him off and Carrunner broke her neck with a hammer blow, and the Blue Jay climbed wailing to the top of the sky.

The Mad Squirrel twitched awake and sat dazed, trying to understand why half of everything seemed to be perpetually hidden. His hand went to his face and pulled back from the eye. It seemed to occur to him all at once what it would mean to go through life blind to half of everything that might attack him. He ran his hand through the vulnerability that wrapped halfway around him. He scrambled in a four-posted circle and ran up the trunk of the tree to the middle branches. Sitting so far above the ground, the meaning of his wound hit him full force. With only one eye, everything was a flat canvas; branches might as well be thirty lengths away as right at hand for all the difference he could see in their depth. The tops of the trees stretched before him, a webbing of infinite danger; the woodlot held out a lifetime of sudden falls and miraculous saves that leave the heart pounding. He must have wondered how many one-eyed spills he would take before he tumbled without a catchplace to the foot of some towering tree.

All the death wish that had driven him was gone. He moved up the tree like an old, sick creature who has been through hard times unfit to mention. Nothing had been won, everything had been lost. The joy that he had felt diving down out of trees on cats, dogs, anything that moved, was gone forever. He would have been a helpless target for the Blue Jay, but the jay had taken his grief to the top of the sky and was trying to fly it off in endless circles.

The Mad Squirrel tried to adjust, but it was no use. He moved timidly down out of trees, craning his neck constantly, chasing himself around in a circle, trying to see behind him and on the blind side all at once. It made him look foolish. Eating made him look pathetic. He dropped half of everything before he could get it to his mouth.

He was an embarrassment to the other squirrels. He must have known how he unsettled the rest of them with his ceaseless watching and jerking around. His vulnerability reminded them of their own. One by one, they changed their feeding times to avoid him. When he was alone, I saw him try his flying leap into the trunk, but it was hopelessly off, and he missed the tree by a body length and fell in an awkward heap.

It was only a matter of time before something caught him running up the trunk because he couldn't see to make that last desperate leap. He must have known that, as well. But I suppose what made up his mind was when Wise Teacher finally came up, quiet as death, on his blind side and stood so close the squirrel could smell the blood on his breath. His desperation came back without the belligerence. He must have smelled that horrible odor coming out of the blind darkness to his right. The odor of CAT!—so close that he could almost touch it, pouring out of his helpless side, out of the arc of darkness—must have been utter terror for him.

There was a tree on his good side and he hunched in a narrow canyon between unseen death and the hope of freedom. Running, he would have been a bloody plaything before he was a foot up the trunk, but a leap was no better than a guess. His body began to pump as if the car that had begun it all had just roared past him again. I suppose he leapt without thinking. The leap was his only alternative.

It was probably not his time to die. The leap carried him a yard up the tree; his hooks clamped the ridges of bark, and he whirled one last time into his slashing counterattack. It drove off Wise Teacher's first thrust, and he did not wait around for the second. He was ten feet up the tree, tucked in the first solid fork. It must have struck him, sitting there, how far he had come down in the world. He had been the scourge of the woodlot. He had been the greatest, the wingless flier, sky-dropping avenger, belligerent prince, death defier. And he must have seen what he had come to—a timid browse with an uncontrollable tic, a paranoid twitch that made him pathetic even when he was doing the impossible.

Wise Teacher cocked his head and watched him walk the endless uphill road of the trunk, then turned away to look for Carrunner. The Mad Squirrel went straight for the top, all the way up the spindly Y of the last leapable branch. There wasn't a branch closer than thirty body lengths when he hurled himself into space for one last free fall.

People who did not see it say that if he had only one eye

and no depth perception, he must have thought the other trees were nearer. But I believe he knew what he had been and could guess what he would become. Rather than die somebody's plaything, he took his death into his own hands.

He hung for an instant out at the peak of his arc, beyond the branch, nowhere near the others. He looked like a hawk spread out against the white blue of the sky, his hands forever stretching for something impossibly out of reach. He fell without a sound, a large, heavy leaf taking the leap.

The Little Dog with the Big Voice

The little Dog with the Big Voice and the Black Dog waged a continual war over who was master of the neighborhood. It was inevitable that it would come to bloodshed and just as inevitable who would win. Everybody knew it but the Little Dog, and perhaps even he knew it but was by his nature incapable of avoiding it.

There was no other competition; the dogs of the neighborhood were all family dogs. Except for an occasional Free Dog who would come across the superhighway and down the avenue on an adventure, they were all householders, landed gentry with slaves who provided the necessities to support their doggy leisure. Most of them had paid for their security with their freedom to run.

Generally the least well fed were also the least strictly watched, but they were all prisoners of the leash, and none of them had the run of the neighborhood. There was too much bickering over territory among the people who lived there for that. A lot of the human conflict centered around dogs running free, their droppings, and their barking—in essence, the same things which occupied such a prominent place in the lives of the dogs themselves.

The most controversial dog, of course, was the Black Dog. He was kept on a chain in a small yard without a fence and he lunged at everything that passed by, on two legs or four. Howler, his owner, was one of those weak, nasty people who buy strength and put it on display because they lack their own. More than one neighbor threatened to shoot the Black Dog if it ever got loose, but no one did. The truck driver next door to Howler once came up to him and shoved a clipping in his face about a watchdog that had gotten loose and had mauled children. I could hear him shouting three houses away. The truck driver had children who were terrified of the Black Dog. The school moved the bus stop down a corner because so many of the children were staying home rather than wait twenty feet from the end of the Black Dog's chain. The police were summoned more than once, but as long as the dog was chained on private property, there was nothing they could do. The truck driver pointed out that the father of the child in the article had shot the dog. He promised to shoot Howler. Nothing came of it. The Black Dog stayed in everyone's life like a reminder of death.

Before I had the enforced leisure to pay attention to such things, all dogs sounded alike to me. But there was a long period when all I had was what I could see and hear from my windows, and the sound of the dogs gave me something to take my mind off the pain and the boredom and the solitude. I listened to the barking of individual dogs until I began to hear another voice, the voice of which all other voices were only a part—the Voice of the Pack.

I did not recognize the Voice of the Pack immediately

although I had heard it once before, while riding my bike in the dirt up beyond the superhighway where the Free Dogs lived on scraps from the dump and what they could run to earth or steal. The voice came up through the trees to the barren spaces where subcontractors had quarried out the dirt and left an amusement park of jumps and curves and downhills. It was a special sound, a crowd of voices with the coherence of a single voice, a unified chorus declaring the purpose of the pack, in which the cry of each individual dog made known its own special function in the action and its status and position in the hierarchy.

It was difficult to recognize the Voice of the Pack in the barking of the neighborhood dogs, but it was there. The only difference was that it came separately, like the notes of a song played one at a time, minutes apart. The periods of silence obscured its unity, but its purpose and its intricacy could be heard by anyone with the time to follow it from hour to hour and from day to day.

I believe that the Voice of the Pack was the voice of the species itself, that diffuse but coherent organism of which each dog was a unique yet indivisible part. Millions of years old, each species is a distinct entity which transcends both the life and the lifetime of the individuals who make it up. Every bird, dog, squirrel, and cat is not merely itself but the expression of an incredibly complex megacreature whose motivations influence the actions of every individual who partakes in its identity.

The long and unbroken chain of doghood's adaptations persists in the genetic inheritance of each individual dog. In every dog lives the contributions of all dogs who have taken part in the chain of which it is a part. In each dog, all dogs continue. The Voice of the Pack is the voice of Dog itself passed on in the genes, and it sings a song of strong and terrible hunters, carnivores, stalkers of prey and eaters of enemies, of social killers continually fighting for their place of dominance or submission within the pack.

In light of their individual lives, of course, the Voice of the Pack was all fantasy and self-delusion. The dogs of the neighborhood had neither the taste nor the aptitude for confrontation that the Free Dogs had; they were dogs who had been born into an easy life and had known no other. The necessity to fight or do deference was a thing for free dogs, who battled daily for new positions in the shifting hierarchy of the pack.

In practical terms, there was nothing to fight over. Each dog had a steady and apparently inexhaustible source of necessities no other dog could infringe on. They were confined most of the time to houses and yards. It could not have been any daily necessity that prompted them to form the hierarchies they did. Some message in the genes must have insisted that, even if they had become apprentice human beings, they should declare their positions in the pack and mark their claims to territory whenever they got the chance. Through the Voice of the Pack, they claimed their positions and issued challenges to back up their claims. Through the ritual of the nightly walk, they marked their territory.

The routes of their communication were inevitable; the culture of their species was inescapably based on the ear and the nose. A dog lives in its nose and its ears. For most dogs, the eyes are for nothing more than noting movement; real information comes in through the hearing and the sense of smell. What a dog claims by voice, it occupies by scent.

Because they were not truly a pack, they had no common territory; and so they left claims to what territory there was as they came in contact with it each night on their walks. Their very passage through a space left information that lingered for hours in a faint but nevertheless identifiable way, but their claims to ownership were deliberate and definite, a series of nose messages no other dog could ignore. They signed their claims in urine and notarized them with the official seal of their droppings, and no conflict of claim and counterclaim was sharper or more irreconcilable than that between the Black Dog and the Little Dog with the Big Voice. The battle between them began long before the Mad Squirrel and ended with the coming of the Lion Dog.

Initially it was a battle of words, or at least a war of sounds. In that battle, the Little Dog with the Big Voice had the advantage; it was something for which his kind had been bred for centuries. The Little Dog was a Lhasa apso, a cat-size bundle of fur with a voice that started at his rear toes and came out like modified thunder. His ancestors had been called Lion Dogs, and they had been temple guardians in Tibet while the Black Dog's ancestors were stealing scraps from wandering barbarians. They were trained for their sharp voice and their ferocity. They were loud, and their quickness made them difficult to kill and thereby silence. It made them excellent watchdogs, and the Little Dog, like his ancestors, made a life out of challenging and harassing trespassers, no matter what their size or species. Everything his kind had passed along the gene chain made the Black Dog his enemy.

The Little Dog had a bit of an underbite, and all that could generally be seen through his mop of beige fur were two large brown eyes and very small, very sharp teeth. He lived with the Old Retired Man and his wife in the small house on the north side of mine, toward the lake. They were a quiet, gentle couple who loved and indulged him like a grandchild. In return, he guarded their house like a temple against everything that walked, ran, or flew within range of his nose or his hearing.

The Black Dog lived south of me, in the house at the corner that faced on the avenue, but he was chained to a steel stake in the ground at the corner of an old wooden garage that faced the street across a short oblong of macadam. Of all the neighborhood dogs, he was the most ashamed of his captivity, and the cries he answered most loudly were the distant, almost muffled cries of the Free Dogs up the avenue across the superhighway.

But his voice was always a little tremulous when he answered them, as if he was not quite sure he could cut it in the face of professional ferocity. It was, perhaps, that strain of self-doubt that made him the bully he was, although it may also have been a matter of environment. Howler was a large, surly man who disliked everyone in the neighborhood, one of those blusterers who make a fist easily but never get around to throwing a punch. The Black Dog had grown just like him. I believe the Little Dog knew that from his bark, and it may have been what led him to make a foolish mistake.

He began by challenging the Black Dog in the barking that went on intermittently most of the day and night. Dogs have a number of ways of deciding who shows deference to whom besides fighting, although that alternative is theoretically available to all dogs, no matter how long they have spent in the softening servitude of pethood. When faced with an obviously stronger foe, a dog will cringe, roll, crawl, whine, fawn, and generally make his surrender as obvious as possible. The matter of who will back down first into those submissive postures is often decided by who can put on the most ferocious show. For dogs who do not often meet face to face, that show comes through the Voice of the Pack.

The Little Dog was one of the smaller dogs in the neighborhood, but he ranked remarkably high in a hierarchy that is theoretically based on the ability to rend flesh. Dogs who passed by sometimes signed the trees in front of his house, but that was a matter of courtesy, like leaving a calling card or a bit of canine gossip describing the vigor, stamina, emotional state, and general health of the passerby. Very few managed to yank their masters off the pavement far enough to obliterate his property markers on the corner of the house, and even the dogs who were momentarily at large did not go up the driveway and leave their claims to territory along his fence.

No one at all went near the macadam strip in front of the Black Dog's, even when he had been left in the house temporarily to tear the legs off burglars while Howler was away. Some dogs signed the register at the mailbox, and a few left notes on the tree across the sidewalk from the end of the driveway, but most left no territorial claims any closer than the far side of the street. After the Black Dog had bolted the length of his chain toward them once or twice, most owners walked their dogs on the far side of the street anyway, and I did not see a dog who strained to get back on the Black Dog's side.

They were not so paranoid when it came to the Little Dog, but they nevertheless accorded him a respect that seemed out of proportion to his size. There were two reasons for this, both of which had to do with the Voice of the Pack. There were two special kinds of barks that determined such things as whose territory it was safe to violate. The first was the kind of challenges a dog made, and the second was the force and timbre of his voice. The first was a measure of his courage and the second a measure of his ability.

The Black Dog was a known quantity—one or two fools had gotten close enough to him to come away bloody—and there was no doubt that the strength of his voice was a direct reflection of the strength of his bite. The Little Dog's advantage was that no one had ever gotten close enough to test him, and until someone could, his challenges had to be taken at face value. In truth, even if he had been allowed to run free, there were not many dogs in the neighborhood with the temerity to challenge a cat, let alone another dog, so the Little Dog took second place in the hierarchy of the neighborhood by default as much as for any other reason.

Nevertheless, he issued some very large challenges. It

was customary whenever a dog came out of a house on a leash for him to issue warnings that he was out and that those who were not prepared to do deference had better be prepared to fight. The coming-out speech was always the loudest bark in a dog's repertory and was often a series of varied warnings. The threat was, for the most part, rhetorical. None of the dogs was that tough, and the chances that one would meet another dog who was not himself bound to a human being by a strap or a chain or the threat of a folded newspaper were slim. The odds that any real fight could occur were small.

Still, all dogs were noticeably quiet around the house of the Black Dog, whether he was out on his chain or not. All dogs except the Little Dog. I do not believe he was quiet anywhere. He started barking about ten minutes before he was about to be walked and continued until he came to the first tree. In addition, he would bark half a dozen times during the circuit of his walk, to let everyone know that he was still at large and it was best to stay out of his way. There was a quality to his voice that convinced me that the Little Dog was not really aware of his own size. His sharp, deep voice had an enormous variety of tones, each of which threatened the various kinds of mutilation a lion-size dog could deal out to anyone who got in his way and didn't bow politely.

Dogs are like samurai: they approach each other like deadly equals, very politely, offering their lineage through their scent and their intentions through their posture and the raising and lowering of their ears. They look like diplomats, but beneath is the courtesy of warriors who are quick to take insult and quicker still to take revenge. The Free Dogs approached each other gingerly at best, and even approached females with caution. The dogs of the neighborhood approached each other as if they were still free dogs. In truth, though, they were more like fat, fifteenth-century burghers wearing the hilts of ceremonial swords in empty scabbards and swaggering to the guild hall. Their barks were formalities and their threats a social fiction.

But the Little Dog thoroughly believed his own threats. He had a cockiness to his walk that was just like his voice, and the one time a Free Dog got near his territory, he ran along the fence on his side trying his best to break through it. If he said in his coming-out speech that he was going to tear the leg off someone and bury it in the middle of the street, he believed he could do it.

Even when he stood in the backyard after dark and shouted threats at anyone who could hear him, he always sounded like he could back up what he said. His voice was not as deep or as loud as the Black Dog's, and even I could tell that he was certainly not as large as the nightmare at the corner, but there was a menace in his voice that came across loud and clear. It was not the spiky meanness of a Pekingese but a true ferocity that derived out of a sense of honor in the old-fashioned sense human beings used to fight duels over. There was a quality in his voice that seemed to say that he was only warning everyone away out of courtesy and would just as soon they stood their ground if they were not prepared to respect his honor.

It was a quality that infuriated the Black Dog. The Black Dog did not bark often, and his bark usually stopped all barking in the neighborhood, unless he was asking for information. He kept quiet, preferring to lie in ambush, waiting for someone to stumble too close to his boundaries. But whenever the Little Dog came out and began hurling threats, the Black Dog was certain to answer in something between a growl and a roar. It was a sound that was always accompanied by a leap against the restraint of his chain.

The difference between their voices was the difference between viciousness and ferocity. The Black Dog's voice promised death; the Little Dog's, stern justice. The Black

Dog's voice was always an intolerable provocation to the Little Dog, and his answer was always a series of barks that crashed out over one another like profanity. The Little Dog always barked last, and if he was commanded to stop, he would growl to himself for a few minutes and then give one last bark to establish who was top dog. It was an insult that invariably sent the Black Dog into a frenzy.

The Old Retired Man never walked the Little Dog south toward the avenue unless the Black Dog was in the house, and he always walked him past midnight, after all the other dogs had been taken on their rounds. But whatever route the Old Retired Man took, the Little Dog was certain to leave his droppings at the point of his circuit nearest to the territory of the Black Dog.

It was just one more outrageous insult in a steadily building chain that reached its peak just around the time that the Mad Squirrel humiliated the Black Dog by raking his nose. The scent of that encounter was like a billboard in the vacant lot to every passing dog. It was a mortification which has few parallels in human society. To have been not only beaten but scarred was a loss of face, but to have been humiliated by a squirrel was almost beyond redemption.

Among the Free Dogs, it would have reduced him to a place in the pack from which he would have had to fight for months to rise. Among the tame dogs, it was merely a topic of gossip. They had all had one or more encounters with the Mad Squirrel, and even the Little Dog would have had to admit that it was not the same as being mutilated by an ordinary squirrel. Still, dogs too are creatures of context, and there was no denying that it was certainly nothing to be proud of.

Nevertheless, no one was going to put that insult under the Black Dog's nose and risk his terrible vengeance. He was certain to get off his chain again, and there was no doubt he would come looking for whoever trifled with him.

The dogs of the neighborhood were dogs of good sense, prudent dogs, and they avoided his territory as always. The bravest of them moved their signatures a few inches closer to the Black Dog's domain, but no closer than they could beg their way out of if they were ever confronted.

Only the Little Dog was crazy enough to rub the Black Dog's nose in his humiliation. Dogs on the scent of something have a peculiar variety of cries that describe their closeness to the prey, their expectations about it, and its identity. Their howls have a different timbre for each kind of prey that is universal. The joyous cry a dog gives in pursuit of a rabbit is totally different from the maniacal sound a dog makes pursuing something that may turn on him at any minute.

There is even a very special cry that signifies to every dog within hearing that the dog making the sound is in pursuit of a squirrel. Even I could tell from the Little Dog's voice whether he was chasing the Blue Jay out of his tree or a squirrel back over the fence. There is a subtle difference, but even the limited hearing of a human being can pick it up.

The first time the Little Dog came out after the Mad Squirrel had torn up the Black Dog's nose, he rattled off a more menacing series of threats than anything he had ever done before. The Old Retired Man almost took him back in the house for fear he would disturb the neighbors. The Black Dog answered him, but there was a muffled, nasal quality to his roars that would have been unmistakable to any dog who had been past the vacant lot and knew the circumstances.

The Little Dog waited patiently for the Black Dog to finish his bellowing, as if he were letting him have the top dog's right of final say. But when the Black Dog had finished, he gave a loud series of barks and a cry that meant "dog-pursuing-a-squirrel." The Black Dog howled as if someone had kicked him and run just outside the reach of his chain. It took Howler half an hour to quiet him down with a series of shouts and threats that could be heard as far away as the Black Dog could.

Every night after that, the Little Dog gave his squirrel cry whenever he came out for his walk and whenever he wanted to end an exchange with the Black Dog. The Black Dog did not answer him after a while, but any time I looked out the window he was always at the end of his chain, straining against it with all his might. The Black Dog's torment would have gone on indefinitely if two events had not occurred.

The first came when Howler went away for the weekend and left the Black Dog in the house to guard his stereo. The second occurred after he came back. When the Old Retired Man took the Little Dog out for his walk, they went north toward the lake, but the far curve of their circle brought them back across the avenue from the south and right past the domain of the Black Dog. The Little Dog trotted alongside the Old Retired Man with the leash hanging slack until they came abreast of the macadam, and then he bolted away, jerking the leash out of the old man's hand.

He went straight for the Black Dog's chain and wrote his name all over it. Then he signed his claims to territory all the way up the short strip of macadam and painted his disrespect on every upright of the garage he could find. At the end of the macadam, he left two solid reminders of his having passed there that were the canine equivalent of the hand gesture a biker will follow a car twenty miles to avenge. He left one just inside the reach of the chain and one just outside it. I believe that if the Black Dog had been there, he would have signed him as well.

But the Black Dog was not only not there, he did not get out until late the following night, long after every other dog in the neighborhood had come by and seen the Little Dog's claims to territory all over the Black Dog's domain. Every dog that went by jerked at his leash to inspect the scene, and each one went away with a little apprehensive sidestep like the sliding back of chairs in a saloon where the gunfighter has just put out his cigar in the marshal's drink. They went by my house with their tongues lolling out and their ears flattened, as if they thought it was the funniest thing they had ever smelled and knew it was the kind of thing only blood could erase.

They didn't have long to wait. When the Black Dog was finally let out, he went absolutely insane. Howler thought it was because he had been cooped up inside for so long, but the Little Dog knew what the ruckus was all about, and he knew who the threats were aimed at. He took them as a personal insult for which he would have to have satisfaction, and the next day he took his opportunity to get it.

He got his chance when the Old Retired Man went to carry some newspapers out to the curb and left the gate open. When the Old Retired Man's wife opened the kitchen door to throw bread scraps out to the birds, the Little Dog was through both openings before anyone knew what had happened. I knew what was coming when I heard the Little Dog's voice pass the gate, and when I looked out the side window up the street toward the Black Dog, I could see him come roaring out of his crouch to the end of his chain. But there was a little nervousness to the way he stood there that made me think he was not so sure of himself after all and was wondering if maybe the owner of that defiant voice was one of those short, sturdy mastiffs who bite deep and never let go.

The Little Dog came around the corner of my house making a sound like a promise to tear off the Black Dog's ears on the way to his throat, and the Black Dog took half a backward step before he saw what was making all the noise. When he did, he did a double-take, and the fear that had been standing the hairs of his coat on end turned to shame and from shame to murderous rage. He strained so hard against the chain it lifted his front feet all the way off the ground.

He was in that same off-balance position when the Little Dog tore into him and knocked him back. But that was the best shot the Little Dog had, and the Black Dog knocked him down and bit him like a barracuda. He clamped his jaws around the Little Dog's middle and shook him like a rat. The Little Dog gave a shriek, but he kept twisting around trying to get a piece of the Black Dog's face or a shot at his ears. I believe the only thing that saved his life was the fact that the Black Dog tried to bite him in half and he had gotten his ribs far enough back in the big dog's mouth to keep him from closing his jaws with all their force.

The Old Retired Man came running up the street and went right at the Black Dog, but there was nothing he could do even to distract him. His wife tried to pull him away from the dogs, but he kept tugging at the Black Dog's chain, trying to make him let go. Probably the Black Dog would have worked the Little Dog forward in his mouth and killed him and then turned on the Old Retired Man if it had not been for the truck driver next door.

He came charging out his back door, and by twisting the Black Dog's choke collar, strangled him into dropping the Little Dog. He jerked the choke collar up until the Black Dog was all but hanging from it, and then jerked him back while the Old Retired Man's wife picked up the Little Dog and carried him away in her apron, crying and trying to stop the bleeding with a dish towel.

When the truck driver finally let go of the choke collar, all the fight had gone out of the Black Dog and he flopped to the ground, trying to get his breath. The Old Retired Man looked at him with a mixture of pity and righteous anger. When he turned away to follow his wife, his eyes were full of tears and determination, and I knew that whether the Little Dog lived or died, the Black Dog's days in the neighborhood were numbered. Even before the old Retired Man caught up with his wife, the street was full of neighbors, and someone took the wife and the Little Dog in a station wagon to the vet. They kept telling her that the Little Dog was going to be all right, but I doubted it.

I was wrong. When the Little Dog got home from his surgery, he had a bandage around his middle and he walked with difficulty. It seemed painful for him even to growl, and it was a full week before they let him out in the backyard. When they did, he didn't seem like the same dog, and I was afraid that the Black Dog had broken more than his ribs. He just stood silently looking around the yard, and when the Blue Jay landed on the back fence, he didn't even bark at it. He just looked at it as if he wanted to run over and show it who was still boss, but he wasn't really sure.

When two squirrels came scrambling down the tree in the backyard, I thought for certain he would chase them away with a torrent of abuse, but he didn't. He just sat down and looked the other way. He looked so much smaller than he had before. I wondered if he had come to realize how small a dog he was under all that fur; small enough to fit in the Black Dog's mouth, small enough to be bitten in half.

After supper, the Black Dog raised his lordly voice to shut up the other dogs in the neighborhood. His bark erupted into a cry that meant he was top dog and he would tear anyone in half who raised a voice to dispute it. There was silence when he finished.

And then out of the silence came a cracked and painful bark that barely carried across the backyards. It was a sharp, defiant cry, followed by the joyous yelp of a dog in pursuit of a squirrel. When I looked out into the backyard, the Little Dog seemed back to his normal size.

The Landlord

The Blue Jay is a romantic at heart; he believes in duty and is willing to sacrifice everything for it. He is willing to kill for it, even die for it if necessary. He has a single rule, which is at the root of all his behavior. He believes he must pass on the property in better condition than he received it; it is a responsibility which it is unthinkable not to carry out. He is the steward of the living complexity that struggles, flourishes, dies, and rises triumphant all around him. His dedication to the property is the cause of his tragedies and the source of his triumphs. It is the most tangible expression of his dedication to the species. Everything he does, everything he is, can only be understood in terms of his duty to the property. The Blue Jay is, first and last, the landlord.

The landlord is on duty every hour of the day, every day of the year. He is there in early spring, when the birds begin to fill the property, fluttering in like the first spattering drops in a thunderstorm. He has seen them leave with the fair weather and he watches the pace of their arrival step up with the orbit of the sun until by April they are a storm of noise passing into the trees like a big thunderhead going over in a slow-motion that runs in weeks instead of hours. The Blue Jay watches them come like a native of the Jersey shore watching the swarm of tourists working its way toward the water as the weather warms.

Having survived on his property through hard times while the tourists have gone off to the ease of their winter homes, he has the superiority a native of any seasonal resort area has over anyone who has not lived there the year around and been tested by its particular bleakness. The Blue Jay collects the rent on his space the year-round. Not even winter is able to drive him off it. He looks at all new arrivals with an arrogance rooted in survival and he harries their stay in his domain from a position of hard-earned authority.

He has not only withstood the winter from which lesser birds fled, he has thrived on it. He has put himself in jeopardy of freezing at least forty more times a year than they have, and he has gained half a year of toughness on them every time they come back. He survives, and he does it with style. What looks like his arrogance is the confidence and the sense of ownership that come with having beaten death in a given locality for a number of years.

He has withstood cold, starvation, predators, and the constant threat of trespassers. He has fought for his space against intruders and has formed a working relationship with those he has allowed to stay and become his tenants. Some have earned a grudging respect from him, and some he is still in the process of driving out, but all have seen winter come and go under his authority, and they are all his responsibility.

But even beyond his obligation to the tenants is his duty to the property itself, and there is no better expression of his love for the property than the oak tree. The Blue Jay believes there should be an oak tree everywhere. The oak tree is more than a symbol for life, it is the symbol for thriving. It says to all blue jays who come after him that the property was owned and operated by someone who improved the lot of everyone who followed. Oak trees are a monument to his management. Everywhere you look, there are oak trees; you can follow a line of them out in every direction. They are way stations, they are hostels for travelers, they are motels for transient blue jays. That is why he plants them, why his predecessor planted them. They are food and shelter. They are Success.

It is not merely on the property that he plants them. He runs them out in strings in every direction from the acreage for which he is caretaker. If he needs to, he can travel for days without fear of hunger and still come back, tree by tree, rest stop by rest stop, to the main, because the blue jay before him and the blue jay before that and the blue jay who was landlord there before the Indians, planted them.

He plants every one by hand; most, he does not even see grow. Ornithologists say he buries the seeds for food and forgets where he puts them, but the Blue Jay is no scatterbrain. He is to the air what Wise Teacher is to the ground. He runs a business here. He is a bird of property. And he leaves it better than he found it.

He operates under the principle that the property is to be passed on to others of his kind. It is a simple biological premise, a basic drive everything but cancer and human beings follow: if the species is to survive, the environment must be improved along lines that favor the survival of the species. If there are to be more blue jays, there must be more oak trees. If there are to be more oak trees, there must be more blue jays. It is a religion with him.

That blue jays break their way to the light from eggs

small enough to lay is a practical matter. But that a tree lies concealed in the rounded oval of an acorn is a miracle worth pursuing. He will tuck as many acorns as he can find into the ground in the hope of seeing that resurrection.

A jay will come back in hard times and root out the godseed and devour it like some apostate committing an act of calculated heresy. A blue jay will eat the potential miracle, like any of us, out of need or desperation. There are few in any species willing to die for faith; the whole idea has no survival value and each species wants, above all, to survive.

The Blue Jay is, after all, a practical, businesslike proprietor. Even a capitalist will live on capital rather than starve. He may have the practicality to store what he needs to maintain the property through the winter and still have a crop, but in a pinch, he will sacrifice the future of the property to maintain it for the present. He has foresight as well as vision, and he knows there is no sense in a miracle if there are no blue jays there to appreciate it.

But that there is more to it than simply putting up stores for the winter can be seen in the way he does it. (I believe it is a religious ritual.) As soon as he lands, he sets the acorn to the right of the hole he is about to create. There may be blue jays who set their acorns to the left—there are sects in every religion—but the Blue Jay always sets it to the right. Perhaps he chooses which blue jays to drive off and which to give the grand tour by determining whether they are right-setters or left, but I hate to think of him as a religious bigot. After all, if anyone in the lot is concerned with matters of dogma, it should be the Cardinal.

In any case, after he sets the acorn to his right, he looks around. Caution is certainly a reasonable explanation, but he would not have landed at all if there were a chance of danger. Besides, there is a way he has of checking right and left for danger that is entirely different in pace and style. The acorn look is more sidelong, as if he is embarrassed at the idea that someone may be watching him at his fool's errand. All he has to go on is faith, and he is a practical, even cynical, being.

Of the hundreds of those small brown promises he tucks under the rug of the lot, only the smallest imaginable number produce a plant, and there is no certainty that the shoots, seedlings, saplings that spring from the spot are necessarily his doing. Certainly an unbeliever, some doubting squirrel or barbarian dog, might point out all the acorns that come to nothing. The vast, vast majority produce no more than a small rumple in the turf.

Probably he is conscious of that every time he cocks his head, always three times, and pokes the spade of his beak into the knot of roots that holds the grass in place, erect and flexible. He works crisply, precisely; with a few slanted thrusts, he chisels an opening. A waggle of the head lifts the mat of grass away from the opening and creates a space in the soft granules of dirt where the acorn can nuzzle in and proceed to grow.

But in between those precise, careful spadings, he looks around and shakes his head as if he hears derisive laughter that such an otherwise staid and conservative administrator could succumb to such an old and ridiculous superstition. Undoubtedly he has good reason to expect ridicule. To the mindless squirrels who disinter his ceremonial offerings, the hiding of usable food in the ground is obvious folly. Only a fool or a bashful benefactor would hide it in a place where even a dog could dig it up. To the squirrels, he must be either Santa Claus or an idiot. Opinions vary.

To a dog, the act is obvious lunacy, and any dog who sees him tuft up the grass and stick that mystery under it will dig it up again just to see what it is all about and go away just as puzzled as before. If the acorn were a bone, the act might make some sense.

Even Wise Teacher considers it an idiosyncrasy at best. He will lift the cover of grass with a hook or push it back with a padded palm to see for certain what is under there, but in the end it is nothing to him but a marker of the spot where some future ambush might be successfully conducted. He has seen it done so many times that he barely uncovers the seed. Carrunner will dig it out, cuff it around like a kitten, and leave it wherever it rolls out of the sphere of his interest. When he does, Wise Teacher marks it for future reference as a place where a squirrel may someday make himself vulnerable.

But you can see from the way the Blue Jay looks around when he carries out his ritual that even if there were no barriers of language and culture, he would not even try to bring truth and light to the cats, dogs, squirrels, or any other tenant. It is after all ceremony that separates the classes and keeps each in its proper station. Besides, it would sound too foolish. What can he say to them except that he is making a tree. There is no way to explain it that does not sound ridiculous, and a landlord cannot afford to appear ridiculous. It encourages the tenants to take liberties.

What's worse, he must bury the acorn right out in the open, away from the tree from which it falls. The ritual requires that it be buried out of the shadow of the tree that will reduce its chances of survival. Generations of blue jays have discovered that no blessings come from the shade. Only hard work in the hot sun produces results.

Even from his own point of view as he nods over it three times before leaving, it is improbable that out of the small, delicious nut come the trees that will sustain his kind on the property long after he is gone. But he buries it nevertheless, and nods his head three times to bless it, looking all the while for scoffers. It's as if there is a litany running through his mind that says, "This is the body of God, eat it and be blessed; bury it and bless others." No matter how foolish he may feel to be backing so unlikely a probability, there is something that tells him that burying it is an act that profits the species. Eating it is an act that profits only himself.

Sometimes he looks around just before he picks the acorn up again, as if he wants to know what in the world he is making such an outlandish speculation for. It's as if the practical, prudent side of him wants to know why he is going to such lengths for a seed he will not even use, except in desperation. Probably he mollifies himself with the explanation that it is simply a low-yield, long-term investment that produces little profit but serves as a hedge against the inflation of winter. Maybe he convinces himself that it's a tax shelter.

Whatever he thinks, he jams the acorn into the pocket he has made for it in the earth and pulls the nap of the grass back over it. Then he cocks his head again and lines up two landmarks, triangulates the exact spot between them, registers the coordinates in his mental files, and takes off, certain in his mind that he has made a savings deposit for himself, certain in his heart that he has made an outrageous speculation for the future of his species.

If he has any remorse, it is probably because he will not be there when the windfall profits come rolling in, when the seed has become a towering observation platform, a hotel for blue jays with food and shelter right at hand. But every time he sits in an oak tree, his mind must feel an earnest admiration for the long-gone jay whose investment has matured into such a majestic and useful tree. His heart must feel a joy in the perfection of the miracle in which he sits, feeds, and keeps watch over the property under his stewardship.

When he has arisen from the ground to the proof of his creed and sits in the tangible evidence of the reward Providence gives to blue jays for diligent effort, he probably forgets the wavering of his faith the ground wrings from him and congratulates himself on both his prudence and his piety. But more often than not, some disturbance

among the tenants or some overdue duty to the property
will turn him back from the heady epiphany of performing
for the species to the simple necessity of keeping his
individual domain from slipping into chaos.

On the ground, the Blue Jay travels by pogo stick, in
body-length strides, leaned back, coming down on the
world with both feet. His head is almost always up,
checking the property, keeping an eye on the grounds.
From time to time, he goes up a floor to the lower hanging
branches to get a new perspective. When he's tolerant, he
watches the sparrows shoot across the lot, trying for the
speed record in the less-than-five-feet-above-the-ground
division. He watches the way a cranky old woman might
forget herself and watch raucous children almost wistfully.
He prefers tenants to be engaged in business, some sober
enterprise that befits the season. Nervous himself, he
dislikes the small, frenetic birds, the chickadees, the
sparrows, the tits, all the constantly in motion birds like
himself.

Probably he resents the way the sparrows keep him busy
trying to make sense of their motions. They shoot low
across the lot at spaced intervals, like tiny jets practicing
strafing runs. The Blue Jay watches them sternly, trying to
figure out what they're up to, whether it should be
stopped, what he should do about it. Sometimes they take
up positions all around the border of the lot and fire at
converging angles toward the center just to drive him
crazy. One no sooner gets his attention than another fires
itself from a branch or the hedge or the lowest point of the
garage roof, streaking at a tangent to the first flight and
snapping the Blue Jay's attention away.

They move his head as if each had a tight wire hooked
over a pulley somewhere above him and connected to his
crest. Each pass stretches the wire of his attention, cocking
his head, rolling it down and right, down and left, jerking it
up a diagonal, tracking it across the sweep of their flight.

Acting together, they make him look like a mechanical bird in a life-size diorama, moving in short, jerky motions like a parody of himself. Eventually he gets annoyed and makes a short glide to the ground to check the nap of the grass or the layering of the fallen leaves.

It's a ruse. He has longer-range plans. The sparrows are short-range birds, with the attention span of children. The Blue Jay can stretch his mind ahead of theirs in time without effort. He knows that if he ignores them for a while, fusses with the improper placement of a leaf or checks the grain of the grass where the obstreperous squirrels have tousled it, they will get bored trying to run his neck ragged and go off to laugh together about the way they danced his snoopy head around.

It doesn't matter where they go. They can clump up on the gravel of the motel parking lot, or take the tickle through their feet on the telephone wires, or rim the bird bath in the Blue-Haired Lady's yard; it's all the same to him. When the last diehard has fired the length of his mission and they are shouting about where to go next and laughing about the way the Blue Jay's head all but twisted off trying to follow them, he will go quietly up to the roof of the tallest tree in the lot. And when they are bunched up conveniently all in one place, he will show them what a strafing run is like.

He knows that once he is out of sight for a while, he has ceased to exist for them. He can afford to wait the rest of the day, going on about the business of straightening up the property until he is ready to give them a reminder of who is landlord and who is tenant. When he has passed completely out of their awareness, they will still be a piece of unfinished business in his, a minor duty that can wait for a convenient time. They are something he can afford to put off. But sooner or later, he will drop on them like a blue hawk and scatter them like leaves.

Or if things are slow and he has the time for subtlety, he

will glide in quiet as a landing owl, slightly downwind, touching his feet to the ground not five feet away from them, where he can intersect anyone he picks out and give the offender a sharp rap on the head in midflight before he can get going. At that range, the Jay can intercept the best darting flight plan any of them can devise. Big as he is, he can outthink them and leave a bloody speck on the crown of any unruly head he wants. The rest will escape, but one of them is bound to dart up the incline of his expectation into retribution.

Pecking and bobbing, giggling and gossiping, they freeze when he settles so close, so unexpectedly. There is always a frozen moment when no one moves. Sometimes he pretends he has only settled there on that dangerous spot by chance. He looks away from them as if his attention is elsewhere. Sometimes he takes a short hop and swings his back to them, tempting them to take off, to explode in all directions in the vain hope, that *all* will escape.

The sparrows are like boys engrossed in some forbidden game, crouched in an untraveled hallway, who suddenly look up to find the principal not two running steps away. I believe sparrows freeze for the same reason boys do—hope and dread: dread that they will be paid back for their flaunting of the rules, and hope that he has not seen them. They stand petrified in an act of faith.

But the Blue Jay does nothing by chance. All reason says he is there to administer his justice, to impress the force of law. But hope says that just this one time it's all a mistake; just this once he will not look back over his shoulder and will go striding off up the air to his office in the oak tree without even a reprimand. And, in truth, he sometimes does.

Sometimes he comes down almost on top of them and lands looking away. I have seen him toy with their terror, taking a short hop one way or the other, taking a second and a third while the sparrows freeze like trespassers.

Inevitably his random hops carry him almost in their midst, but they stay still, watching the focus of his attention, which he carefully directs away from them across the lot. He has all their moves covered. He has the authority and the temperament to enact some punishment, to exact some toll for their temerity.

Having flown into his space, they are subject to his justice. He is the equivalent of federal law; his territory overlaps their individual and collective areas; his rights transcend theirs. His position is commanding. They are no longer at scoffing distance from his justice. He is close enough to pass sentence. They watch him like defendants cowering before a hanging judge.

When he has worked himself that close, tying them in tighter and tighter knots of terror, he will sometimes turn his head slowly toward his shoulder. The sparrows stop shivering and tense for flight. There is a perfect awareness between them. The error of their ways is inescapable, his superiority is undeniable. The carefully coordinated flight plans that made him the butt of their joke look like the plots of children next to his strategy. They look foolish and inept. Alone, he has maneuvered them into puppetry. The simplest turn of his head plucks the wires of their fear; he is in control, he has the power. All they can do is hope for mercy.

When there is no doubt that he has snared them in an intricate web of action too complex for them to do anything but tremble at, he gives a ruffle of feathers and flies off without looking back.

Blue-Jay Justice

Revenge would have been too puny a motive for the Blue Jay to have done all the things he did to make the death of his wife and their brood a landmark in the life of every tenant. As always, he acted for the species.

At least one member of every species who passes through his property will have an unforgettable altercation with him, one that warns of even greater guile, ferocity, and power to come. He leaves the same message with each species that comes through his territory: "Look out for the one with the black mask and the blue coat!" He impresses that message on a single individual, with the knowledge that that individual will carry the memory and the message of their encounter into the winter and will pass it along in his song. All winter long, he will sing it as part of his summary of what he has experienced as part of his species.

Bird, dog, cat, or human, it is the Blue Jay's aim that each should have an experience of him to pass along to others of their kind. Ultimately he wishes to have a warning about himself broadcast in their genes; he wants to be the legendary guardian of his space, the flying menace everyone around is born with a warning about. It is not a matter of vanity; that kind of reputation simply keeps the tenants on their toes and cuts his work in half. More important, it will make survival easier for every jay who comes after him.

One stunning victory over a well-respected member of a species will allow him to let others pass freely across his land with only an admonitory skirmish or two. But the dogs he must harass constantly just to keep them in line. He has raised a knot on the Black Dog's head and has buzzed the Little Dog with the Big Voice innumerable times. But they are such enthusiastic creatures that they forget who is boss a day after he has shown them. The cats are different. He has a working alliance with the cats; they share information. He has a respect for their abilities. They are even his deputies on the ground at times, and he will direct their investigations from above, calling their attention to a particular intruder or oddity on the ground. But they are more mercenaries than allies, and they will turn on him and devour him if he is careless enough to give them the chance.

The actions of the Mad Squirrel made squirrels another matter. The Mad Squirrel cost the Blue Jay dearly, and all squirrels were forced to pay a dreadful price for it. He lost a generation of offspring and his sole hope of passing on the genetic transcription of what he knows. All squirrels were doomed to pay for that as long as the Mad Squirrel lived. Their sentence was fixed. It was an escalation of hostilities designed to show them the ante by which his vengeance increases. He had a wife and children. He took three squirrels for each.

Three is his number; it is his expression of infinity. He understands things in threes. All larger quantities are understood as functions of three. When he stores seeds, he counts them in sets of three. When he buries an acorn, he fixes its location in three dimensions. The Mad Squirrel cut off his potential in time in threes, and he took his vengeance in multiples of three. It was a terrible thing to watch.

When the Mad Squirrel invaded the Blue Jay's nest, he cost all squirrels a protector and paid them out with an enemy. For years, the Blue Jay and his wife had warned the squirrel community whenever one of its young went beyond the bounds of safety. His wife would shriek warnings to every squirrel mother in the lot if any youngling was poised on the edge of a leap beyond its capacity.

In payment for his wife's death, the Blue Jay let two young squirrels plummet to their deaths without making a sound. The first tottered on a branch for a full minute before it went hurtling to the ground. Perhaps his incessant cries could have called some adult to its rescue. I believe the Blue Jay thought so, because he waited until it hit and then set up a racket that drew a half-dozen squirrels out onto the branches. He shouted his name at them, a sharp, mocking *jaay! jaay! jaay!* as he rose into the air.

I did not see the second fall, but I heard the Blue Jay's din as the cats poked at the rolled ball of fur beneath the tree, and I knew his implacable vengeance had destroyed it as surely as if he had struck it from the branch himself. I believe the squirrels knew it as well, because thereafter there were always two or more adults around any of the youngest squirrels, and even young adults were watched continuously. It forced him to turn elsewhere for his justice, but he was not short of opportunities.

The life of anything that lives that far above the ground without being able to fly is precarious at best. The Blue Jay had only to wait for the hazardous moment and every squirrel was his. Not a day goes by that some squirrel does not face a situation that could be fatal. In half of those, the intervention of the Blue Jay could be the difference between life and death. He took his third victim at one of those points where the width of a squirrel's hand span is the difference between the leap made and the final fall.

Just as the squirrel made the short leap from one branch tip to another, the Blue Jay flung his weight against it, landing on the very tip and pulling it down out of the clutching hands that reached for it. I know it was not a matter of coincidence, because he simply pulled the branch down and away and then let it go. He landed on another branch closer to the ground and stayed there until his cries had brought out the whole squirrel community to witness his retribution.

He took the fourth at the same place, with a con-centration-shattering cry at the crucial instant that sent it tumbling into that irreversible stillness into which his wife had disappeared. He had made his selection carefully—a young adult not entirely adept at such leaps, whose concentration was vulnerable to the distraction of his raucous cry in its ear. The squirrels began to look for him constantly, and they set up a chattering chorus whenever he was around. But they needed him nevertheless.

His weight just beyond the fulcrum of crossed branches could catapult them into the necessary-but-impossible leap. Hundreds of times in the past he had performed such services for his tenants, landing at just the right place to counterweight the swinging fulcrum of a curving branch or leaving, in the nick of time, the branch a squirrel needed next. His spring-deadening weight at the root of a branch from which a squirrel sprang could drop any of them into the abyss. He had them looking over their shoulder at every aerial crossroad for fear he would land out of nowhere and reverse all their careful calculations in mid-leap.

But they could not avoid the dangerous transitions from tree to tree entirely, because the bounty dropping from the branches had made the cats step up their patrols on the ground and made travel there even more dangerous than ever. The Blue Jay became a scourge in their lives, and he drove them into a panic that had them terrified to move. They were like middle-class householders locking their doors and staying in because there is a maniac on the loose. Their travel in the higher branches ceased almost entirely, and they went from one tree to another with a caution that was almost fanatical. He had them afraid to live their daily lives, and when they were conscious of how much they needed him in the trees, he turned his attention to the ground.

His fifth victim perished while slipping past the Black Dog as it lay drowsing between her and a tree. Halfway there, too far inside the circle of the Black Dog's chain to escape, the Blue Jay's accusing voice called her doom down on her as she tried to sneak carefully by. If a squirrel was in a vulnerable position anywhere, he blew the whistle on them. Wise Teacher watched him continually, knowing the Blue Jay would tip him off to a juicy strike sooner or later. The Blue Jay used the cats for his justice, but even they must have known that he would turn that same wrath on them eventually, and when he did, it was worse than anything he did to the squirrels.

He executed the squirrels with sound and he executed them with silence. The sixth forfeit his justice levied took a male on the ground who was carelessly ignoring his back in the delirium of finally found food. His silence covered the stealth of Wise Teacher's approach as he came stepping perfectly from behind and pounced suddenly and without warning. But the voice that was silent while Wise Teacher stalked the squirrel brought its death to the attention of every squirrel within hearing. His racket showed them clearly how much they had profited from his watchful eye before the Mad Squirrel had made all squirrels his enemies.

I believe the squirrels understood what had turned the Blue Jay against them, because they tried to disassociate themselves from the Mad Squirrel by refusing to feed when he fed. When that did not curb the Blue Jay's wrath, they raised a racket every time the Mad Squirrel was on the ground and vulnerable, as if they hoped Wise Teacher would kill him or at least hurry him into the trees, where his one-eyed flight might tumble him to a natural death.

I could always tell when the Mad Squirrel was on the ground by the curses hurled at him by every other squirrel in the lot. His willfulness and his radicality had been only an annoyance when they had exiled him, but when his madness brought ruin to the whole community, as they had warned him it would, the squirrels were ruthless in their response. I believe they would have lynched him and left his body hanging from the Blue Jay's nesting tree if they could. They did the next best thing, and tried to harass him into an early demise. In the end, it was probably some Judas squirrel whose antics drew Wise Teacher and Carrunner to the lot the day the Mad Squirrel died.

Day by day, all squirrels felt the subtle squeeze of the Blue Jay's might. He made the branches too dangerous to travel and the search for food on the ground a form of suicide. But it was not vindictiveness on his part. It was an absolute necessity to impress on them in terms so strong they would never forget that they should never, under any circumstances, allow a blue jay to come to harm. But I do not believe he took any joy from the slaughter. I believe his mind kept going back to that stillness into which his wife had vanished, stopping his voice in the middle of his song.

Only the struggle to administer his justice sustained him in his grief. Each day, he kept himself alive by striving toward burning that warning into the genes of every tenant on the property: "Never harm a blue jay!" It was a message he was forced to write in the blood of squirrels to make a lasting impression. The survival of his kind depended on it. It was his obligation to the jay who would take over the property when he grew too tired and too foolish to hold it and disappeared into imprudence and that unforgettable stillness. He owed that much to his species; it was an imperative that transcends grief. His duty kept him alive.

The landlord of any place is a blue jay. He must make sure human, dog, cat, bird, and squirrel know who is landlord and who is tenant. The Blue Jay's methods were direct. Notices about death were written in blood. His warning to both cats and dogs would be written in the blood of Carrunner. He was to be smashed in such a way that it would strike terror in the nose of any dog who came near the spot where it occurred for as long as dogs kept their running record of events on every stationary object on a common route.

No dog who was a witness would be able to leave a general message without the tremor of having seen a blue jay cause such destruction. The dogs of the neighborhood would bark about it for a long, long time, until the youngest dog to be able to detect that occurrence at its faintest recognizable point had grown old past remembering, until it became a legend about blue jays that would keep the unruly dogs in line for his successor and the successor of his successor.

The property had been given to him in order, and he was obliged to pass it on the same way. But the same duty that demanded the destruction of Carrunner required the preservation of Wise Teacher. Whatever his personal grievances against the Seal Point, Wise Teacher was a source of information for the next jay and the kind of challenge that would insure that only a strong jay would be able to make the place prosper. Wise Teacher was a necessary adversary to keep the next jay sharp, but he was also a tool. By checking the deviation from routine in the rounds of Wise Teacher, any jay could save himself the time of having to investigate the whole route himself. Wise Teacher was both his gift and his curse to his successor.

Just as the Blue Jay wrote his warning to the cats in the blood of Carrunner, he wrote his warning to the humans. I believe he was as aware of his human tenants as he was of the rest, and I saw him scold more than one dog owner for letting a charge run loose. He had seen the interaction of one human with another and knew whose cries would establish the wrath of blue jays in the understanding of humankind. I think he would have destroyed the Blue-Haired Lady for that reason even if she had not owned Carrunner, by making sure she witnessed his destruction.

Maybe he knew that with a gift of flowers, she would work her way close enough to tell me her horror and her sadness, and I would include it in my song about what it is like to be part of the species for all the winters left to me. No doubt my cast anchored me in front of that grief for some cosmic reason, but the Blue-Haired Lady was a hard case to watch the shock wave of that tragedy shatter.

This is the message the Blue Jay sent by way of her: "Terrible is the vengeance of blue jays! In humans, they break the ones who shatter easiest!" Anyone who had nothing to do but watch out his window could have counted the days of the Blue-Haired Lady's decline from that terrible accident. She did not survive Carrunner by more than a few months.

Catcall

It may have been hubris that destroyed Carrunner, the madness of overwhelming pride the gods are said to strike kings with before they rip their lives apart and leave them broken examples for the rest of humankind. In mythology, the avengers of the gods have wings, so it is probably no coincidence that it was the Blue Jay who struck Carrunner at the peak of his pride and brought him lower than death.

Why he should have picked Carrunner rather than Wise Teacher has no basis in justice. He could, sooner or later, have destroyed both, or perished in the attempt. I believe he did it the way he did because Wise Teacher was an asset to the property, a source of information he had to leave to his successor. But Wise Teacher was also a test to make sure only the fittest of jays took over so valuable a property.

It may also have been that grief had begun to wear away

at duty so much by then that the Blue Jay took the first good opportunity he saw to put the property back in order before he left. He would have been a long time waiting for Wise Teacher to give him a perfect opportunity, maybe years. Carrunner gave him a good opportunity at least once a month. That was an average; if things were tense between Wise Teacher and Carrunner, if he had humiliated himself in some foolish way before his mentor, Carrunner would regain himself in the only way he could. Because he lacked prudence, he had a surfeit of courage, and whenever he had lost face, he went to the wheels to get it back.

It was not very long after the Mad Squirrel took his own exit that Carrunner made his crucial mistake, and, in fact, it was the Mad Squirrel's last escape that triggered it. It was the breaking point between Wise Teacher and Carrunner and it fell together like a row of dominoes, one event knocking over the other. It was one of those experiences that make everyone involved immediately begin to catalog all the tiny and seemingly inconsequential things that could have made it come out differently. That seems to be a habit of people in the face of tragedy, to reconstruct the event and change the details that led up to it one by one.

Wherever there is unexpected blood, there is always a human being saying, "If only . . ." If only Wise Teacher hadn't been so curious, everything might have been different. If only he hadn't paused that extra second on the blind side of the Mad Squirrel trying to figure out the limitations of being blind in one eye. If only he hadn't tried to test the boundaries of the Mad Squirrel's limitations, the squirrel wouldn't have had that extra second to make the leap that set him free to make his own end.

But Wise Teacher knew the squirrel was dead meat sooner or later, and he could afford to wait and see what would happen. I believe he lingered there with his whiskers almost touching the Mad Squirrel's blind side just to see what would happen when the squirrel realized his jeopardy. Maybe it was because he could feel the shadow of coming events that the handicap fascinated him so much he let the prime moment go by and shamed himself in Carrunner's eyes.

I believe he paused there with his whiskers touching what was going to happen, not quite close enough to see how to avoid it, but close enough to know it was coming. I believe he froze in the grip of a premonition that something dreadful was going to occur, something too close to avoid. The hackles of his fur rose just before the squirrel bolted, and I believe that he could see the workings of the Blue Jay's revenge in a misty, shadowy way and it stopped him short.

Maybe it was just curiosity, or maybe the fact that the squirrel showed no fear whatsoever made him overly cautious. Maybe he didn't understand that the squirrel couldn't see him, didn't have a clue that he was there, right on top of him. Maybe he thought it was another unorthodox trap hatched by the squirrel's madness. Maybe he didn't even know that the squirrel who had sat so stupidly, so close to the claws, was only a remnant of the squirrel who had dropped out of the trees on him and driven him off the block.

Certainly the Mad Squirrel was nothing to be taken lightly. It was easily conceivable that he had been playing cripple for so many weeks waiting for a chance to lure Wise Teacher into the circle of his rage long enough to do him damage, as he had with the Black Dog. Perhaps it was caution that made Wise Teacher hesitate. Wise Teacher was a student of the odd detail, and perhaps the squirrel sitting there like something waiting to be taken was too much like a trap.

He had edged Carrunner over toward the tree for precisely that reason. If there was a trap, Carrunner was sure to leap into it, and he had put too much time into his apprentice to put him in a position where his foolishness could get him hurt. He had seen what those sharp, small hooks had done to the Black Dog, and he had no desire to carry a half-blind apprentice for the rest of his life.

He had a responsibility to Carrunner that was part of the contract. He was responsible for the Blue's education, and although it was necessary to put an apprentice through some difficult tests on his way to true learning, Wise Teacher was still responsible for seeing to it that the worst Carrunner got for foolishness was a few lumps that would teach him a lesson. Naturally there were dangers that he could reasonably expose Carrunner to, but there were others, like the Mad Squirrel, for which there was no precedent and which he was required to handle himself.

Besides, the squirrel was a deepening puzzle, and finding him sitting at the bottom of the tree like that, sort of dazed, as if he was brooding over a misspent life and wondering what there was left to live for, was just the most recent mystery in an expanding chain. There had been an absentmindedness in the squirrel that had been gathering for days like the darkness of a storm. In the middle of a meal, he would freeze as if he had forgotten what he was doing. Even in the trees, he would have lapses of action that could not be traced to any difficult transition from the tip of one branch to the tip of another.

I believe that he would be running up a branch flattened and distorted by his blindness and would suddenly realize that it was a branch he had run up a thousand times when he had been at his peak. It was mostly in the locust tree that those stillnesses would catch him. They would freeze him on the spot in mid-stride as if he was suddenly plunged into some moment when he was climbing up that trunk toward a kamikazi dive on some unsuspecting passerby. I believe that for a moment, he was truly there again, with the road of the trunk stretching up away from him toward the sky in three dimensions just as it had always been. His pace would quicken for a moment just before he froze, as if he was suddenly seeing the close-up landscape of the tree as it had always been.

I believe that what froze him was not the sudden breakthrough into three dimensions but the sudden fall back into two. I believe it was the plunge back into a black-and-white world out of the brilliant color of memory that stunned him and made him so still. The pause, where he stood with a foot raised, poised, just about to hook into the bark, was always longer than the upward flurry that preceded it, and after the stillness, he would always go on up the tree more slowly and cautiously than he had before.

When he paused on the ground, I believe that he had picked up some nut from the past and, mulling it over in his hands, had suddenly seen it round again instead of flat. It was probably that flash of sensation from his memory, more real than anything around him in the suddenly distorted world of his new perception, that had covered Wise Teacher's approach and it was probably the sudden, stunning realization that he was back in the limited world where everything was wrong to his senses that stunned him into inaction when he knew that Wise Teacher was there.

I doubt very much that it was pity that held back Wise Teacher's hand; at best, he would have simply made the killing quick out of respect for what the squirrel had been. Almost certainly, it was caution and curiosity that held him from raking the squirrel behind the ear and ripping him forward with a snap of the wrist. Hesitation was the prudent thing to do; if it was a trap, caution would keep him free enough of it to escape, and the information he gained about the squirrel's true limitations would help him predict any future traps. It was like going into enemy territory for reconnaissance.

Probably he had just come to the conclusion that the squirrel was no threat and was about to spook him toward Carrunner so the young cat could get some practice, when

the squirrel made the intuitive leap that left Wise Teacher
with a paw foolishly raised a fraction of an inch from where
the squirrel had been.

It would have been an easily covered lapse if Carrunner
had been in position. But he wasn't. If only the Orange Cat
had not been in heat, he might have been in position and
what happened later would not have happened. But she
was, and she was moving on the outskirts of the action as
she always did, picking up at a distance everything Wise
Teacher was showing Carrunner. She stayed silent, moving in the shadow of the motel at the far border of the lot
until Wise Teacher maneuvered Carrunner in a wider
circle away from the squirrel. Then she rolled on her back
and gave a quiet cry that jerked Carrunner's instincts in
the same direction as his nose. It drew him in a wider arc
than he should have followed, and he wavered between the
attraction of the Orange Cat's display and Wise Teacher's
unspoken command. He stopped halfway to his station and
hesitated, then turned off toward her. But when he was far
enough out of position, she suddenly stopped her display
and shot through the gap in the fence near the lake end of
the motel and was gone.

Carrunner turned back toward his duty, but it was too
late to do anything but watch the Mad Squirrel make his
leap to freedom. If he had been in position, the squirrel
would have been his. He should have gone out at a wide
angle and then come back with the tree between him and
the squirrel. He should have waited just around the curve
of the trunk so that when the squirrel made his leap for the
tree, he could have swung around and smacked it to the
ground as soon as it hit the bark.

But the squirrel was gone and he was standing dozens of
lengths away from his purpose, and there was nothing left
but the assignment of blame. Carrunner had the advantage
there; he had been making his excuses all along as he
drifted toward the Orange Cat, and he was ready. In the

moment after the squirrel made his blind leap to the tree, while Wise Teacher cocked his head in befuddled surprise, Carrunner made his point.

Siamese cats speak Chinese. They have a language of inflection, where a sound can mean a dozen different things depending on the variations in its pitch and its context. The sound that Carrunner made came close to the sound of human derision a two-bit hustler makes when his sucker misses the eight ball on the lip of a pocket and there is nothing between him and the money but half as many racks as he can run on his worst day. It is the sound a biker makes when he goes by some weekender with a bright new bike who cut him off halfway around a berm and then took the rest of the banked turn too fast, went up over the back of it, and stalled out. It has no words, and it is not a laugh precisely, but it is full of scorn and derision, and I have seen bikers punch each other silly over it.

It is a communication between males of every species that is only tangentially connected to sex but has something to do with the right to reproduce, with the fitness to carry on the species. It is always a challenge, and it is invariably made by someone who feels his own claims to reproduction have been bettered. In short, it is the sound a fool makes out of his insecurity, and it is answered only by fools who have their own doubts to put to rest. I believe that is what passed from Carrunner to Wise Teacher. It was an unmistakably human sound, and what it said quite clearly was that Wise Teacher had been afraid, that his fear had held him back, that he was too old to take the right step, that his wisdom had made him cowardly. It was a sound that said, "Scared of a half-blind squirrel! And you have the nerve to call yourself a cat, a master of the hunt! You have the nerve to try to teach *me* what it's all about?"

It was a revolt Wise Teacher must have been waiting for a long time—a little sharper than he had expected, a little more hostile, but a challenge he knew had to be coming.

But he was not Wise Teacher for nothing, and he took it in his stride. I thought he would stalk over to Carrunner and back him down with a hiss and a swipe of the claws that would draw blood. You would think all that hard pavement would have taught me better.

But Wise Teacher was secure in his superiority. He seemed to shake his head in a way that said, "You ought to learn to keep your mind on your work," and walked away, leaving Carrunner with the choice to follow or end the apprenticeship and go off on his own. There was a surety in the unhurried way Wise Teacher walked that said that while he was willing to continue the teaching of such a foolish and inept apprentice as Carrunner in the hopes that his monumental foolishness could eventually be overcome by disciplined training, it did not matter to him whether Carrunner followed or not.

It was not arrogance, nor was it bluff; Wise Teacher simply knew who he was and what he was worth. He was the best there was and he was getting better. Neither praise nor derision could touch him. He was beyond anyone's opinion but his own, and his opinion was that there was too much more to learn to waste time on trivialities. He had no need to fight. He had assessed the situation and knew its outcome. Nothing more was necessary. I believe both of them knew it.

Perhaps if Wise Teacher had dodged a few of Carrunner's best swipes and raked him once across along the flank, things would have turned out differently. But Wise Teacher had his own distractions; the puzzle of the squirrel hovered just beyond his comprehension and filled him with apprehension. There was something of old age and death and helplessness in the way he walked that was a direct result of that enigma. I believe Carrunner mistook Wise Teacher's preoccupation for weakness, because his voice rose to the level of direct challenge, and they moved away from the tree with the dispute still between them.

Carrunner's voice got louder, but Wise Teacher ignored him. There was more fear in it than indignation, more uncertainty than rage, and it was obvious that Wise Teacher knew it. I expected him to rush Carrunner and drive him off, but he sat down instead and began to lick his paws as if he was saying, "You are a fool. If you persist, I wash my hands of you."

The Mad Squirrel dropped between them like a stone.

The body bounced, rolled, and lay still. Wise Teacher prodded him with a paw and touched his whiskers to the fur where it was matted and broken. The bristles on his fur were up, as if he had touched a mystery greater than death. Carrunner ignored the squirrel. His voice was loud and defiant. Wise Teacher looked at him over the body for a moment, as if anyone who could ignore so great a mystery was ignorant beyond redemption. Then he turned and walked away. They must have dissolved their contract at that moment because Carrunner turned and walked away as well. And they were not together after that—until it was too late.

Heat of the Moment

About an hour after Carrunner went into business for himself, he was still in the lot. He had taken out all his anger on the grass and had raked the bark off the big oak the Mad Squirrel had fallen from. Nothing seemed to help, and I knew where he would be going next, to make a dash toward his death so he could come away triumphant. I believe he would have gone to the avenue right then if the Orange Cat had not come back through the gap in the fence near the motel. She gave a cry that was almost a plea for relief, and yet she seemed to avoid Carrunner, moving toward the street along the fence and the garage at the north edge of the lot.

But she did not get all the way there; she stopped in the lakeside corner of the lot and gave another half-whine, half-shout. The voice was not her voice but the voice of the species, crying out in pursuit of its necessities. The need was not really hers either, but she clearly felt it no less keenly. She sat down and started to wash, but she couldn't keep her mind on it, and she got up and paced back and forth in a tight elipse like she was stopping short of the walls of an invisible cage.

Carrunner had stopped scraping bark off the tree, but he did not make any advances. No doubt he was afraid she would bolt away again, and he had learned enough patience from Wise Teacher to make a show of indifference. For her own part, the Orange Cat seemed oblivious to him as well, and she kept up her tight, anxious pacing, shortening the loop every time until it was hardly more than a step in one direction and an immediate counterstep in the other, as if she could not make up her mind which way to go.

I believe it was her natural independence that made her take the step to run and the irresistible force of her hormones that made her take the counterstep to stay. She looked like she wanted to jump out of herself, and her eyes had a haunted look. Every movement she made seemed to be tightening its way down into a twitch. She sat down and got up and sat down and started to wash herself and gave up and stood up and sat down like her skin was growing too tight for her body.

Carrunner strutted obliquely toward her in a sort of angular course that might take him close to her but not in a direct line she might run away from. He was strutting again and stalking at the same time. The Orange Cat took a second step in the running-away direction, but there were forces holding her where she was. No doubt whatever cat had come by at that moment would have been drawn into her event as inevitably as she was. There was something moving in the lot that was beyond any two individuals; it was the need of the species itself to go on.

Probably some other mixed breed would have been

preferable to her. She did not seem to find Carrunner beautiful, and yet something was clearly shoving her in his direction. Carrunner had a male cat's single-mindedness on the subject. It was his biological commitment to make more cats as often as possible. He had not come to Wise Teacher's reserve and never would. Perhaps the species worked differently through each of them, and Carrunner was the expression of its tendency to mix the gene pool. If any cat anywhere was in heat, Carrunner was distracted, and if he missed making his rounds with Wise Teacher, there was no doubt where he was.

He had no standards except quantity, and he seemed to have no preference for his own particular kind. Siamese seemed no more attractive to him than Angora, and I believe that if he had come across the Cheshire Cat in heat, he would have mounted it. It was probably the odor of heat itself that was irresistible to him, but what drove him was the species's own need to provide a wider variety of cats as a hedge against destruction. Whatever the traits of his polyglot offspring, none of them was the same, and if there was a genetic advantage to crossing one pool of genes with another, Carrunner provided it.

Probably each individual animal is born with a genetic predisposition toward one strategy or the other, either the preservation of a pure strain or the variation of the strain. Each approach has its survival potential. What has worked in the past would certainly seem worth passing on to future generations. Wise Teacher's intelligence would have been a gift for all catdom, and there were not many circumstances where it would not have helped the survival of any of his offspring who had it.

Still, there have no doubt been times in the evolution of cats when Wise Teacher's meticulousness, his natural prudence, would have been less useful than Carrunner's recklessness. When times are hard, survival often means taking new, even irrational, risks, and there are times when immediate action is more important than studied decision, times when it is better to leap than weigh the consequences.

Nevertheless, most difficult times reward the conservative, the prudent. Probably for that reason, creatures like Wise Teacher have one grand passion, which comes inevitably with the optimum chance to enhance the species. For Wise Teacher himself, it was the one female who had a pure strain of intelligence to match his own, a Seal-Point Siamese called Purrfect Moving Mind. What drew him to her and her to him was a matter of chemistry, a precisely shaped molecule of odor that fits in the brain like a key and unlocks the passions.

For creatures like Wise Teacher, there is only one mate, picked out for him by the unfolding plan of the species. And so that he and his perfect mate will not miss each other, they are born with an irresistible attraction for the scent of a unique and specific set of chemicals. Each has both a scent and a preference no other living creature can duplicate. Their pairing is inevitable, if they pair at all. That they should come together was inherent in the first pair of Siamese.

When Seal Points first became a breed of their own, countless as the possibilities were, every combination of traits that could be made by arranging and rearranging that limited pool of genes was there. Probably there was no plan that said this combination of genes will become Wise Teacher and will combine inevitably with the combination of traits that will become Purrfect Moving Mind in so many generations. Probably there was no cosmic matchmaker who said Wise Teacher will be born and will mate only with Purrfect Moving Mind. But from the first Seal Points, there was a potential that the exact combination of traits embodied in those two cats would come together.

Individual as they were, they were only the manifest destiny of Seal-Point genes working itself out, a permutation which got to become real while so many other possible combinations remained only theoretical. From the instant Wise Teacher became a living, breathing combination of traits and Purrfect Moving Mind became the embodiment of her genetic inheritance, they began moving toward each other.

There were probably a million ways they could have missed each other, and the fact that their single combination managed to complete itself was a miracle in itself, but no other pairing would have been possible. In Wise Teachers of all species, whose number is extremely small, there is always an irresistible bonding into *specific* pairs. If the best of a certain trait is to be crossed with the best of another trait, creatures like Wise Teacher and Purrfect Moving Mind can have no completion except in each other. They must be destined for each other through a chemistry inherent in their genetic makeup to pass on their perfectly interlocking traits for the good of Seal-Point kind.

Still, if all cats were Wise Teachers and Purrfect Moving Minds, a single catastrophe could wipe out all catkind in a single generation. But the species does not risk its continuation on a single strategy; it pursues, with equal intensity, a general mixing of traits which are not so exceptional as those of the Wise Teachers. All the obstacles to the evolution of cats have not yet been encountered, and there is always a need for innovations to meet the unexpected.

Thus there must be a strain within the species who have a different kind of attraction, precisely the opposite kind from the Wise Teachers. To mix up as many groups of traits as possible in the hope that at least some of the numerous innovations will be useful in the face of uncertain and unforeseeable conditions, there must be Carrunner's kind of attraction. And although at any given time, the proportion of Wise Teachers and Carrunners will vary, there will always be both and there will always be cats.

Carrunner's function was to mix Seal-Point genes as widely as possible through the population of all cats. His attractions and the attractions of others like him, male and female, were superficial, intense, and temporary by necessity. If the scent of love brings the Wise Teachers and Purrfect Moving Minds together and holds them long enough to produce a mix, there must be the scent of lust to bring together the Carrunners and Orange Cats of the world to meet, mount, and tire of one partner after another and stir up the gene pool with their thrashing.

Carrunner was a perfection of that tendency. His attractions were neither deep nor selective; there was no way they could have been if his obligation to the species was to be met. The chemical attraction that drew Wise Teacher drew Carrunner just as strongly, but it drew him infinitely often and in every direction from which the wind blew. If there was an opportunity to leave a mix of traits, Carrunner was incapable of passing it up. He was impulse itself, the strain of action that the species needs as a defense against times when intelligence is of little value. When times are bad, when there are disasters for catkind everywhere, when so many that are born die despite their uniqueness, there is no time for the slow, single selection of one Wise Teacher for one other.

Neither Wise Teacher nor Carrunner was aware of what drove him, but each was as helpless before his drives as the other. Wise Teacher could no more have walked away from Purrfect Moving Mind than Carrunner could have walked away from the easy access of the Orange Cat. Nor could the Orange Cat have turned away from the pattern she had inherited. No single-minded pairing could have produced a mixed breed like the Orange Cat, no drive toward careful selection. Nothing in her genes pointed toward selectivity. The Orange Cat was like Carrunner, caught in a drive that allowed no personal preference. Her heat twisted her with an unscratchable itch that gave her no peace, and Carrunner could keep his mind on nothing else while there was an opportunity to scratch any itch, anywhere, in any cat of any kind.

I doubt that Carrunner or the Orange Cat even liked each other, but when the fit was on each of them, proximity was all that mattered, and the compulsion that held the Orange Cat to her spot in the corner of the lot drove Carrunner toward her just as strongly. What came together in the lot, public and commonplace, was not two individuals but the needs of the species twisting two individuals to its purpose. What strutted toward the Orange Cat was an irresistible impulse, and what waited for Carrunner was an undeniable necessity.

The Orange Cat kept twitching between leaving and staying, between arching and enticing Carrunner and running away. Carrunner dropped his pose of disinterest as soon as it was obvious that the Orange Cat no longer had any choice. The flood of her chemistry was at its high-water mark, and she had no control of herself. Carrunner could have been any cat; what the Orange Cat needed was to be mounted. Her identity made no difference to Carrunner, either; there was only the irresistible need to release the insufferable tension.

There was none of the elegant courtship of Wise Teacher and Purrfect Moving Mind; there was only an immediate and irresistible attraction. The closer Carrunner came, the more inevitable their joining was. Their noses drew their brains and their brains drew their bodies. Their coupling was short and intense, more like an attack. It was all yowling and thrashing, like two necessities being squeezed into a common space. From a distance, it looked like mayhem, it sounded like murder.

The shrieking rose to a crescendo and burst into silent indifference. Carrunner sat back and began to clean his paws. The Orange Cat walked away, as if someone else had performed the spectacle. She began to trot, and a few yards away, she lay down on her stomach and nuzzled over in the grass, as if she was relieved that it was over and she was herself again. Carrunner went on preening himself for a while, but he did not leave, and the Orange Cat went no further away than halfway across the lot.

There was an inevitability to that, as well. For associations to be many, encounters must be brief, but in their short space of time, there must be repeated attempts. Carrunner's kind are driven together, a helter-skelter mixing that may or may not take. In an hour, the Orange Cat and Carrunner might be miles apart, unlikely to meet again, and the opportunity for the species to mix those dissimilar genes would be lost. In a few moments, the Orange Cat's necessity would be gone, and Carrunner would be dragged along another scent with no time to look back.

They lay apart for a few moments before the Orange Cat's urge began to build again, twisting her with its force. The tension brought her up to her feet, made her arch and stretch. Carrunner shot across the grass toward her. They came together like combatants, wrestling for position, and after a flurry, they separated like commuters leaving a train where they have been pressed together. Carrunner walked only a few steps and sat cleaning his paws, but the chemicals that drove the Orange Cat were waning, and by the time Carrunner had caught his breath, she had lost interest and had gotten up to walk away without looking back.

Carrunner was after her in a flash, but she turned on him and what had been mutual necessity moved toward rape. The sounds were shrill and violent, and they tumbled over and over. Out of the rolling argument, the Orange Cat came up running and fled across the street toward the avenue. Carrunner was up and running after her, taking huge, rolling strides full of an intensity that was partly sex and partly rage. He overtook her at the far side of the street, but she dove under a parked car, and he prowled around it waiting for her to come out.

She lay under the car complaining in the cracked, screechy tones of her particular accent. Carrunner paced and argued in demanding, forceful tones. The Orange Cat's noise came out from under the car like appeals, but they were futile sounds and Carrunner seemed to count them no more than an aristocrat in any century would count the protestations of a peasant wench complaining against what was clearly his by the right of his birth and gender.

He tried to crawl under the car with her, hoping to pin her down, but she bolted out from under the front bumper, and he had to crawl the length of the car before he could come up out of his stalking crouch and into a full run. It gave her a ten-yard head start, and she turned the corner of Carrunner's lawn at full speed. It was probably only the headlong tilt of her flight that saved her life. She shot along the macadam and past the little garage well within the stretch of the Black Dog's chain.

The Black Dog had gotten up from his lounging position on the edge of the macadam a dozen times during their argument under the car and had dragged his chain to full length to peer down the street. But he had walked back to his favorite place and had just lain down again when the Orange Cat came tearing around the corner of the fence. Surprise kept him lying there, and by the time he could leap up, she was already past him and gone, back along the narrow, weed-choked passage between the old garage and the fence.

Carrunner should have been able to see him through the thin wire fence, but his motion was not his own and the momentum carried him around the corner in hot pursuit. The abruptness of his stop defied the laws of physics, but it did not keep him from coming whisker to jowl with the Black Dog. They seemed to press up against opposite sides of an unbreakable pane of glass for one long moment.

It was undoubtedly the worst nightmare of Carrunner's life come true. I believe he thought he had come to the end of his life that had haunted his sleep like a premonition through all his adulthood. I had seen the nightmares come on him while he lay stretched out in the warm summer sun. I had seen him roll to his stomach and crouch there like a kitten waiting to be pulled from the jaws of death by its mother as he came fighting slowly up out of the dream. He always came awake with a squall that rang with the sound of teeth gnashing together in a kitten's face.

The Blue-Haired Lady said it was because when he was a kitten, his curiosity had taken him almost inside the circle of death marked off by the length of the Black Dog's chain. His mother had jerked him away just as those ferocious teeth were about to close over his head. It must have marked him for life until greater traumas erased the mark.

Whatever kittenhood memory came back to him in sleep, it came again and again and seemed to linger as a reality for him for hours after the nightmare passed. I believe he thought that the dream of death and the reality of death had finally merged.

But the element of surprise was on his side as well. The Black Dog had come out to the end of his chain to sniff at the trail of the Orange Cat, tracing it to the corner of the fence to assure himself that it had really happened, that he had had one of the enemy so close to his grasp and let it slip away. He had turned his head toward the garage and was just swinging it back toward the street like a shovel at the end of a crane when Carrunner blundered into him. The sheer unexpectedness of it happening twice left him stunned, and it gave Carrunner a chance to spring backward, tumbling over himself and rolling just out of reach.

By the time the Black Dog reacted, Carrunner was up and running, and the nightmare teeth snapped at empty air. He did not stop until he was at the lake at the far end of the street and halfway up a tree that hung out over the water. Perched on the branch, he looked like the Mad Squirrel, and I could see the adrenalin rush working its subtle magic on him. If the Black Dog could have gotten close to him again, he would have run away in a molasses of slow motion. But the tide of adrenalin ebbed, and I could see him thinking it all over and wondering what it had been worth. I do not believe he paid any attention to the Orange Cat when he saw her again, and by the time she was in heat again, tragedy had rearranged his priorities.

Purrfect Moving Mind

Wise Teacher was the opposite of Carrunner. If the female was not a Seal-Point Siamese, he had no more interest in her than if she were a dog. He was an aristocrat who found no attraction outside his class. The tendency of the species to keep a pure strain motivated him, and he was immune to the lures that distracted Carrunner from almost anything else. Because he had a narrow field of interest in mating, he was not distracted by every opportunity that passed. It was probably the source of his intense concentration, his ability to focus objectively on what was going on around him.

It was not that selectivity made his drives any less intense; it simply made them less diffuse. If anything, his passions were more relentless than Carrunner's once he had found the perfect mate. There was a Seal-Point female in the white three-story house directly behind mine. She was a show cat, and her owners kept her close as harem guards. I believe that when she was in heat, they took turns sittng up with her for fear she would learn to unlock the front door and let herself out. The husband would come out on the back porch and forcibly drive off any cat whose nose had drawn him into the vicinity. He had a BB gun and was not above shooting at cats that would not be frightened off by a shout and flailing arms.

They had a large kitchen window that faced my backyard, and the only time I ever saw that cat was when she was in heat. She would come to the window and lie up on the ledge and press herself against the glass. I would see her there almost constantly for about a week, and I was certain that soon the backyard was going to fill up with male cats and Mr. Catkeeper would be out with his BB gun, popping away at the most compulsive Romeos.

Carrunner had to be whacked away from the back door with a broom, and there were about a dozen others who would come and set up a wailing chorus half the night sometimes. All that ended one night when about twenty of them were milling around near the back fence. The place looked like a locker room after a big game when Mr. Catkeeper came out and tossed something backhanded out into the middle of their convocation. The closest ones had already started to scatter, but those further away whose glands had the better of their reflexes moved a little more slowly, until the firecrackers started going off. Then they shot for openings in the fence slats in a rout.

I am sure Mr. Catkeeper thought he had driven them away for good, but he was wrong, because they were back by moonrise; what drove them off for good was Wise Teacher. He had come to investigate and had seen the one correct silhouette on which he was imprinted. He had excellent taste. I had seen the cat's picture in the paper. She was something of a local celebrity, having won some fancy New York cat shows, and if there was another Siamese worthy of mixing her perfection with Wise Teacher's, she was it.

Her name was Purrfect Moving Mind. It was a pun on a Chinese name or some Oriental philosophy, the kind of joke people with Ph.D.s who insist on being called "Doctor" would appreciate. She would arch and stretch in that window like a mixture of queen and call girl. She would rub herself against the glass in a way that seemed to ache, and if she looked possessed by passion to human eyes, I cannot imagine what she looked like to Wise Teacher. She must have looked spectacular, because the moment he saw her climb up into that window with the light of the kitchen on her like a spotlight, he turned on the rest of the would-be suitors like Ulysses come home.

A Siamese has more range than a coloratura and more voice tones than an Academy Award–winning actor, and Wise Teacher used all of them. The first sounds out of him tempted me to shine a flashlight into the neighbor's yard to see if it was really him. For sheer loudness, it beat the Little Dog with the Big Voice, and for force, it surpassed even the Black Dog. When I first heard it, a shiver ran down my spine that must have been genetic memory, because the image that flashed through my mind weighed six hundred pounds, had four-inch teeth, and became extinct none too soon for my cave-dwelling ancestors.

It must have conjured up some awful images for his competitors as well, because more than half of them left without checking to see where they were going, and about six came flying through my backyard like the Black Dog was half a step behind them. I suppose they might have stayed around if it was anybody else but Wise Teacher. It was like one of those movies where the strong-silent-hero-who-doesn't-even-wear-a-gun suddenly walks into the saloon, throws a glass full of beer in the gunfighter's face, and gives him thirty seconds to get out of the state of Texas.

It certainly astounded me that that sound could have come from Wise Teacher. I had heard him make more sounds than a five-year-old child, but the most violent of them would have to be classified as stern. The noise he made that night was unthinkable. It was like Dr. Jekyll turning into Hyde; a smoother, more elegant gentleman than Wise Teacher did not exist, and suddenly there he was standing in the middle of a dozen dockworker cats, looking like a Hell's Angel speed freak halfway through his second bottle of cheap wine.

The cats that didn't instantly find something better to do just sat there, somewhere between stunned and amused. I believe Carrunner thought he was kidding, but he knew how fast Wise Teacher's hands were and he wasn't going to get close enough to find out. Wise Teacher looked at the fools who had stayed behind and gave them a second warning that would have curdled the blood of a demonologist, and another quarter of them left on more important business, while the rest backed off to the fence and looked like they were just trying to find their hats and coats and would be gone in a minute.

Only one of them stayed where he was, and as far as I could tell, he was a stranger. Cats do not seem to be much different than human beings; there is always one fool who will stand where he is, in the face of certain destruction, to defend something he does not want all that much in the first place. The cat who stayed was a big tom, black and white with a lot of British longhair in him. He looked about twice the size of Wise Teacher, and he hadn't even begun to erect his fur and make himself bigger.

Wise Teacher was sleek and muscular, but a Siamese looks like a good light-heavyweight at his biggest, and the strange cat looked like he fought in the unlimited class. I expected some sort of conversation, a sort of shoulder-shoving exchange of voices, but Wise Teacher's second cry was the last sound for a full minute. The strange cat flexed his fur, and he looked like something there should have been bars in front of. Wise Teacher doubled his size in an instant. I know rationally that an adrenalin rush simply made his fur stand up, but it was still a spectacular sight to see.

For a second, it looked like a Mexican standoff, and I thought they would just face each other down unless the stranger took a backward step; but I was wrong. Wise Teacher picked up his left foot and put it down like a karate master walking on rice paper without leaving a mark. After that, it was just a blur. If the strange tom had had any sense at all, he would have changed his mind as soon as that foot came down, but he started forward. He raised his own foot to take a step toward Wise Teacher, but he never got to put it back down.

There were a lot of shadows in the yard, but the two cats came together where the light from the kitchen window made a slanted square of light like a boxing ring, so it wasn't a lack of light that made me miss most of it. Wise Teacher seemed to move from one side of the square to the other without transition. One instant he was putting one foot forward, and the next, he was all over the tom.

There was a double scream of cat voices making the kind of sound you have to check twice to convince yourself it isn't human. It's a sound full of sharp edges and ragged tears, things being ripped and rage and pain. If there is a sound in everyday life that anyone would recognize as the quintessence of violence, it is the sound that filled up that slanting square of light.

Wise Teacher and the tom seemed to merge into one cat, and I could see Wise Teacher digging with his hind feet like he was making a hole in that cat big enough to bury himself in. They were a dark shadow spinning and rolling in the air for a moment, and when they hit the ground, the strange tom came shooting out with nothing more on his mind than a place to hide and the feline equivalent of medical attention.

But Wise Teacher must have been holding that anger

back for a long time, because he was on that tomcat's back before he could get to the rear edge of the light, and I could see real tufts of fur come flying out on either side of Wise Teacher like he was pulling the stuffing out of a pillow. They passed right out of the light and into the darkness of the yard, and what seemed like a half-second later, the tomcat came screeching through my yard and down my driveway, gaining speed the whole way.

When I looked back, Wise Teacher was walking back into the square of light and there was nobody else in the yard except a few fight fanatics who had crept back to the far side of the fence. About half a second after he stepped into the light, Wise Teacher turned on them, and the sound alone would have been enough to leave them bloody. In less time than it could possibly have taken, Wise Teacher was the only cat on the block, and the next day and any of the days that followed, he was the only cat that came near that place, including Carrunner. In fact, there was a distinct scarcity of cats in general in the neighborhood for as long as Wise Teacher's courtship lasted.

But with the need for violence gone, Wise Teacher's intellect returned, and he could not have needed it more. The object of his attention was still locked up in a big three-story tower with guards who at least thought they were as smart as Wise Teacher. Still, smart as he was, I do not believe he would have gotten in without the help of Purrfect Moving Mind.

With the competition gone, Wise Teacher settled back into his usual silent watchful self, but there was a difference. His rounds were quicker, almost perfunctory, and more and more of the neighborhood seemed to be left to Carrunner as Wise Teacher spent more and more time prowling my backyard and making nighttime inspections of the White Castle's defenses. Mostly he tried the obvious entrances; he tried the cellar windows, but none of them was open or broken, and then he tried the doors, but they were never left ajar.

The only time Purrfect Moving Mind came out, she was on a leash and Mr. Catkeeper was on the other end of it with a long stick whose purpose would have been obvious even to Carrunner. Nevertheless, Wise Teacher followed them wherever they went, never more than a few steps back, and he and Purrfect Moving Mind carried on a conversation which seemed to consist of outrageous proposals and demure rejections. But from what happened afterward, something promising must have passed back and forth between them.

To me, it didn't seem like anything could be done. The White Castle was locked up tight, and there was no way to get even a window open as far as I could see. Wise Teacher checked them all out carefully just the same. There were two big window air conditioners on the ground floor and another one on the second, and he managed to get up on one by way of a garbage can. But it went on while he was standing on it, and he made the long jump to the ground rather than take that vibration tickling his feet.

For two days, Purrfect Moving Mind stood at the window painfully looking out, and Wise Teacher prowled around the backyard looking up wistfully at her. Then on the third day, she was not in the window anymore, and I assumed that her ardor had cooled a little earlier than usual and her hormones had carried her back into disinterest before they could get together. But I was wrong.

I could still hear her yowling vaguely from inside the house. It was a near incessant racket, and it must have driven the Catkeepers crazy. But there was something very odd about it. First of all, Purrfect Moving Mind had always been remarkably quiet for a cat in heat, due no doubt to her breeding. In the whole time I was aware of the attraction of cats to the White Castle, I barely heard her. She seemed to allow herself one plaintive cry every day, but after she disappeared from the window, her racket was more or less constant.

Then on the second day of her absence, Wise Teacher

began pacing back and forth across the back fence almost continuously. While I watched him, I noticed that the sound of Purrfect Moving Mind seemed higher up and that I could hear it far more clearly. For a minute, I thought she had somehow managed to escape, and it was only after I looked out twice and was sure that she was nowhere around that I realized I could hear her because the top of the attic window had been lowered.

Apparently she had gotten up into the attic by yowling in front of the attic door until it was opened. Cats are inscrutable at best, but under the kinds of stress heat brings on, they are crazy and any behavior seems understandable. Apparently the Catkeepers let her up into the attic and then opened the top half of the window to give her some fresh air when she refused to come down. No doubt they were glad to put up with any idiosyncrasy for a little peace and quiet.

As soon as the window was opened, she yowled for about five minutes to let Wise Teacher know where she was and then shut up. For security, she might as well have been in the Tower of London. The window was just under the peak of the roof, and there was a little roof about a foot and a half wide under it that ran across the back of the house like a sort of high crosspiece on a huge capital *A*. There was another roof over a little back porch, but that was a good twenty feet below, and the rest was sheer slats of white siding a fly would have had difficulty climbing.

The Catkeepers went back to their routine, secure in the knowledge that Purrfect Moving Mind was safely and quietly sequestered in the attic. I don't know whether it was in desperation or just as a feint to keep their minds off the attic, but Wise Teacher made a spectacular attempt to break in about suppertime the day they opened the attic window.

He waited alongside the house until Mr. Catkeeper came home from work and then walked right up the steps behind him, quiet as a shadow. He could have gone in with Mrs. Catkeeper a half-hour earlier, but I suppose he thought she was too observant. People almost never look down when they walk into their own houses and clever dogs or cats can slip in or out anytime they wish. Mr. Catkeeper was no exception, and both he and Wise Teacher disappeared into the house together. But before the door shut completely, I heard Mrs. Catkeeper scream, and there was a commotion during which I imagine Wise Teacher overturned some furniture, dodged some lethal blows, and shot back out of the house with nothing gained.

Actually he had gained quite a lot; probably exactly what he had intended. From then on, the Catkeepers' attention was riveted on the downstairs doors, and just to make sure that's where it stayed, Wise Teacher was skulking by the side of the front porch when they went out to go to work the next day. After that, he was with Purrfect Moving Mind.

How he accomplished it was a feat in itself. She had managed the really clever part in getting the window open; all that Wise Teacher had to do was get himself through the top half of a window three stories above the ground. I watched him do it with my heart in my throat. The first third of it was easy enough—for a squirrel.

There was a big maple tree in the backyard with a limb that stuck in over the slanted part of the main roof. Wise Teacher went up the tree toward it like a telephone lineman, digging his sharp, curved hooks into the bark and hunching up the long trunk to the first branch almost inch by inch. It was a hell of a climb, probably the equivalent of a human being scaling a six-story building, but he went right on up.

The branch that shot up at an angle over the roof forked out from the main trunk about twenty-five feet up and gave him as easy ascent most of the way. He walked up the incline as calmly as if he was walking on the fence. But the limb narrowed, and by the time it got over the roof, it was about an inch thick. When he got to the tapering end, I was hoping he would see that it was too dangerous and come back down, but he didn't.

The branch divided and narrowed sharply above the roof, and he had two choices: either go out on a branch a squirrel wouldn't trust and step off about an inch above the roof much nearer the peak, or stop where the branch was still thick enough and make a three-foot jump onto a sharply slanted set of shingles. He stood at the fork of the branch for about five minutes before he finally decided. He made the leap.

He hit going uphill, but there wasn't enough traction to keep him from sliding backward down the roof. He tried to dig his claws in, but his leap gave him too much momentum and he went sliding for the precipice. I thought he was finished.

But his back feet went into the rain gutter as he got to the edge, and he stopped with his hands dug into the shingles of the roof. He stayed where he was for a full minute, crouched and trembling. Then he got himself together and climbed up out of the gutter. It must have been filled with wet, old leaves, because he stood on the roof and shook each of his feet off, one after the other, with the short, flicking, step-shake-step-shake motion I had seen him make whenever he first came out into snow.

He walked across the slope of the roof toward the back of the house until he came to the edge. I believe he made the climb because he was smart enough not to look down, but when he came to the edge of the roof, there was no way to avoid it. The little cross-roof intersected the edge of the main roof about two feet up from the corner, and all he had to do was step carefully down from one to the other. But it must have been like stepping into a scaffold halfway up the World Trade Towers. The cross-roof was a lot less slanted than the main roof, but it was narrow even by cat standards.

I know he must have thought about what that fall would be like, because he tucked his legs under him and sat on the roof looking down for a good two minutes. He always pulled his feet in under him like he was hiding his cards from prying eyes whenever he had a weighty decision to make. But finally he stuck one arm out, very gingerly, spread his fingers, and put the soft pad down on the gritty shingle of the cross-roof all in one long, slow motion. As soon as the pad touched, he raised himself up on his other three legs as if he was stretching himself and put his other hand down.

He kept his arms stiff, as if he was testing how much slide there was to the roof. Then he carefully brought his left leg forward and over the lip of the top roof. He put it down almost on top of his left hand, and then he brought his right leg forward and did the same thing. When he was finished, I could have put my palm under all four feet and lifted him.

He lowered his body down over them and sat there to keep his momentum from starting him on another slide that there would be no rain gutter to stop. He sat perfectly still for a minute, waiting for all possible momentum to die away. Then he turned slowly and stretched himself out in a long panther stride across the roof. The walk to the window, once he got himself going, was relatively easy. The roof was not flat but it was far less pitched than the peaked roof, and once he had overcome the momentum of stepping down and was sure he would not landslide over the edge, it was as easy as his walk up the branch. But at the end of it was the most dangerous part of all.

The window was short and narrow, and the top half of it was down only a little wider than the thickness of his own body. He stopped directly in front of it and tried to figure out how to get in. Very gingerly he put his hands up on the sill. It was plenty wide enough, but it did him no good. Then he walked his hands up the side of the frame, but the higher they went, the more dangerous it got. Stretched to his full height, he might easily tip over backward, and there was only a foot and a half of roof to catch his balance in. He stretched his arms up one side of the window and then the other. But it was no use—the opening was still too far above him.

Purrfect Moving Mind came to the glass and looked out at him. She looked at the window from corner to corner. Then she stretched up and hooked her hands over the top of the frame and dug her claws in. She lifted her feet and hung on it. For a moment, it did not budge, and then it dropped four or five inches all at once. She twisted and fell backward off it and out of sight. But in a moment, she was back up on it again. This time it did not move at all.

The window was still not halfway down, but it was a lot lower. Wise Teacher stretched his arms up the side of the frame again, but it was still too high. He knew it, and she knew it. The east face of Everest could not have looked higher or more unscalable than that window, and Purrfect Moving Mind gave a cry of despair and desperate need. I suppose that is what made up Wise Teacher's mind, although it must have been apparent to him that even if he went back across the little roof and climbed back up onto the peaked roof, there was no way he could get back to the tree.

When he had made that leap, he had committed himself fully. There was no way back, and from where he sat, there was no way forward. Purrfect Moving Mind pressed against the window and *miaaowed* plaintively. Wise Teacher squeezed his eyes together and twisted his head to the right like he was forcing himself to an irrational decision. Then, inch by inch, he backed toward the edge of the little roof until his tail was hanging over the edge into the abyss.

He moved his front feet back like a spring-loaded catapult, hesitated for an instant, and then sprang for the opening. It was a one-way jump. If he did not get a good part of himself through, no number of lives would have saved him from that long fall. I can still see him straining upward, frozen for an instant at full length, his claws out, his skin stretched tight from elbow to hand, giving the cry of pure will that carried him halfway through the opening.

His arms went through, and for a second it looked like they would fail to grasp anything and he would come sliding back out, but he hooked his elbows over the frame of the window and scraped his feet on the glass for a foothold to push himself the rest of the way. It seemed hours that he hung there, struggling against the gravity that threatened to yank him back out the window and fling him down to his death. Finally he hunched his shoulders one after the other and squirmed himself further up until his left rear foot hit against the frame and pushed off. I saw him drop down over the other side of the glass and disappear.

About an hour later, he was back looking out, his face pressed against the glass, looking down. He looked like he thought it had been worth it. In a few minutes, Purrfect Moving Mind came up alongside him, and they sat there in the window, washing themselves meticulously and looking down from time to time at the fortunes and misfortunes of the world. Then Purrfect Moving Mind rubbed against him, humping her back up under his nose as she moved across his face, and they went away from the window again.

Later in the afternoon, they were back, and they stayed longer, but they went away again and came back twice more before suppertime. The last time I saw them there that day, they suddenly sprang away from the window, and I looked at my watch and realized it was suppertime and the Catkeepers were probably coming in the front door. I waited, listening for shots and expecting to see Wise Teacher's body come flying out the back door, but there was nothing except Mr. Catkeeper shaking his head over the way the window had come down and pulling it back up into place.

I imagine there are a hundred places to hide in an attic if no one knows you're there, but none of them solved the problem of getting back out. I looked up at the window from time to time for the next couple of days, and each time they came back to the window, they looked more content and more relaxed. By the third day, when they sat washing themselves, their movements seemed to flow together in a single motion to which each contributed half, like an old married couple finishing each other's sentences. Sitting in that window, they were the quintessence of their species; they looked as if they would never be separated again. But cats are not citizens, and about an hour before the Catkeepers came home, they sat there for the last time together.

What happened after that is conjecture, but I suspect that they made love one last time and then came downstairs, with Purrfect Moving Mind going first to see if the coast was clear, and Wise Teacher moving with that strong, silent step behind her. Probably they moved like scouts dropped behind enemy lines, in silent single file toward a rendezvous with the submarine, until Wise Teacher was hidden behind the couch.

When it was time, after supper when the dishes were done, I heard Purrfect Moving Mind howling, but the howling was far away at the front door. It started just a second before Mrs. Catkeeper opened the back door with the bag of garbage. She put out a bag every night after supper, like clockwork. I should have known Wise Teacher would have filed that away before he went in.

I suspect that while Purrfect Moving Mind scratched and wailed at the front door, and Mr. Catkeeper got up to look out and see if that damned Siamese Seal Point was on the front porch again, Wise Teacher slipped out from behind the couch and made a soft, quick run to the kitchen. I doubt that he stopped at all, because as Mrs. Catkeeper opened the door, he shot out between her legs and into the backyard.

She let out a shriek when she saw him come bolting out of nowhere, and the garbage bag went flying, but it did not seem to strike her until he was halfway across the yard that he had been coming *out*. She stood there in the doorway screaming Mr. Catkeeper's name and cursing Wise Teacher, who, well out of reach, trotted to the fence and looked back over his shoulder in a way that said that what she was doing was not only poor sportsmanship but in incredibly bad taste.

There was an instant when I thought Purrfect Moving Mind was going to follow him out the door, but she got to the doorway only in the arms of Mr. Catkeeper, who clutched her to his shirt as if he thought she was perfectly safe. Wise Teacher turned around at the fence and gave a cry that was part defiance and part joyful exultation, and it seemed to finally dawn on Mr. Catkeeper what his wife was screaming about. He shouted something after Wise Teacher, but I did not hear what it was because I was laughing too hard by then.

The Wheels

Carrunner and Wise Teacher prowled the same territory
for the rest of the summer, but they always came and went
at different times, as if they had agreed to do so, and
whenever they were around at the same time, they were
always half a block apart. But as Wise Teacher withdrew
from the territory in pursuit of Purrfect Moving Mind,
Carrunner began to treat most of the neighborhood as his
own, and when Wise Teacher disappeared into the White
Castle, Carrunner abandoned the careful schedule they
had worked out between them and came and went as he
pleased. When Wise Teacher returned, confrontation between them was inevitable.

When the conflict came, it was over in a flash. Carrunner was loud and abusive. It seemed to have something to
do with the place where the Mad Squirrel had landed, but

it may have been that that was simply where their paths finally crossed with no way back. Carrunner bristled and shrieked; Wise Teacher smacked him behind the ear the way a mother would discipline a kitten. I don't believe he even extended his claws, but the blow snapped Carrunner's head around, and it was so quick that he could not have gotten out of the way even with a week's notice. It humbled him utterly. It said clearly that Wise Teacher was so far beyond his skill that a fight was out of the question and they both knew it. It was true not merely because Wise Teacher was quicker than Carrunner but because he knew every move his ex-apprentice could make and was a dozen steps ahead of him.

It was clear from the way he struck that he knew exactly how long Carrunner was going to carry on before he made his move. He knew to the second when Carrunner would stop berating him and attack. He waited until the last instant and moved first, while Carrunner was still puffing himself up and trying to find the courage to strike. There was complete silence for a moment, and then Wise Teacher's voice cracked the air, sharp and strong and angry. It sounded like a large, square blade falling in a chute. I believe he said that he would tolerate no more of Carrunner's foolishness. Either the Blue would live in the neighborhood unobtrusively like the other cats, or Wise Teacher would drive him out. Carrunner said nothing. When Wise Teacher finally walked away, there was no question who was master of the ground.

The Blue Jay watched them both from the big tree from which the Mad Squirrel had made his final leap. Carrunner stayed in the lot long after Wise Teacher had gone. He paced back and forth without going anywhere. Once he stopped and tore up the grass, silently, like a child throwing a tantrum who's afraid he is going to be heard by parents who have had enough of his temper. I watched him trying to eat his humiliation, and I saw it stick in his throat. I knew where he would have to go and I knew why. I had seen it happen before. Whenever he lost face with Wise Teacher, he would go to the avenue and test himself against the wheels. It had always been the one method he had to keep his self-respect, the one instance where his mastery was equal to Wise Teacher's.

I watched him walk along the street toward the avenue. I had seen him do it twice, and when he stood, rubbing his back along the big tree near the sidewalk at the end of the street, I knew what he was going to do. He would rub himself on that tree for a while, crooning softly to himself, and when he was ready, he would streak toward the white line at a sharp angle that would take him right up against the wheels of the fastest car that came along.

Down the avenue, the road curves over a little cement bridge across the lake and then straightens out for half a mile or more of irresistible speedway. When I heard the motor start to climb toward a roar, I knew he had picked his car. I knew exactly what he was doing because I had done it myself, riding the speed limit down a narrow road behind a ten wheeler. Sometimes, when you have swallowed your self-respect one time too many, there is nothing to do but swing out blind around that house-size back end and into the oncoming traffic with your throttle twisted past anything but final commitment.

You have to swing out around that blind corner, passing the truck at seventy, and kick down into fourth so that when you pass the cab you can be going eighty, if there isn't something coming the other way. Sometimes you have to swing out into the face of death to get the stains off your life.

I did it more than once, almost as many times as Carrunner flung himself toward the wheels. The road opens to your vision like a moving doorway, and sooner or later you find, filling that empty oblong between the truck and the far shoulder, the road and the sky, the square face of another ten wheeler hurtling toward you less than a truck length away.

There is nothing you can do then except twist the throttle and shoot forward on the blind hope that you can get through the alleyway between the two trucks. But even if you make it, the wind bending forward from the truck you're passing and the fist of wind from the truck that is coming the other way are going to smack you from both sides. If you are very lucky, the leading edge of one wind and the trailing edge of the other will hit you equally at the same time, and you will wobble and slide back into the right lane, topping ninety.

When your desperation carries you into that narrow space where the rush of two huge billboards of metal blot out the sky on either side of you and the world shrinks to a little corridor whose rushing walls skim past you close enough to touch, you come to a point where your fear drops away and there is only your concentration and your skill. If you let your focus waver in the slightest degree, the force is going to slam you against the side of one truck or the other and you are going to go down in a mangled heap, sucked under the rear wheels or into that space where the undercarriage and the cement will grind you like hands crumbling cheese.

But in that instant, everything slows down and the grime of your defeats washes off you and the world lights up and you see more clearly than you will ever see again. When Carrunner's whiskers touched those spinning wheels, I knew he was seeing the white-gold epiphany of the world that comes when the mundane goes translucent and shimmers with a brilliance beyond description.

I knew the indescribable joy he felt when his skill carried him into the orbit of death and out again into a world risen again, whole, perfect, and beautiful beyond words. I knew what it feels like to shoot through, timing it so perfectly that you hit the front corner of the truck you are passing at the exact moment you hit the rear corner of the truck passing you and the two sudden slaps of wind hit you simultaneously, and you squeeze through the funneling backwash and back into the right lane ALIVE! ALIVE!

The car was not visible at the end of the street when Carrunner shot out from the tree, but I knew exactly where it was. The Blue Jay knew it, too. I saw him leave the lot only a second or two before Carrunner flung himself toward the avenue. The car came past the tree as a white blur.

I could see all three paths converging, irresistibly drawn to the center of the event. Time slowed way down, almost stopped. Wise Teacher turned the corner of my driveway. He moved as if the event was winding him in on an unbreakable line. He froze with his left front paw lifted from the ground and his ears pointing forward toward the intersection of the street and the avenue. The Blue Jay stopped in the middle of a wingbeat, his beak pointing toward the inevitable. Carrunner was stretched out at the speed of light in mid-stride. The car was a white streak passing beyond comprehension.

If I could have drawn a straight line from Wise Teacher's eyes, the tip of the Blue Jay's beak, and the center of Carrunner's forehead, they would all have come together at the same point not a micron apart, converging at the exact center of the car's hubcap where everything spun too fast to see in the rotating wheel.

Then everything snapped loose and seemed to slide forward, the bird and the cat and the car all coming together at the exact same point. I believe that if eternity has a physical location, they had centered on it, and they fell toward it like stars pulled by the inescapable density at the center of a black hole.

Carrunner was a ball of concentration. I knew exactly how he felt. He was going between trucks at the limit of speed, and all there was in the world was him and that narrowing gap between his ability and utter destruction. The closer he got, the more I could feel my bike under me, the buffeting bodies of the trucks as they went by in opposite directions on either side like giant hands shoving me back and forth. I wanted to look away.

But my eyes were strung on the same converging lines as Wise Teacher's. That old absolute terror came roaring up out of my stomach, shaking my bones to splinters. I could feel it winding out like the high whine of a bike disappearing into the distance. And then it was gone, with a pop, into the absolute lack of fear that comes at the fulcrum of the frozen moment. I was with Carrunner at the moment when his concentration replaced his need, when his discipline pushed out everything but the moment. From the tree to the point of imminent impact, he was Wise Teacher's equal. He was totally aware, completely in control, betting his life on his courage and his skill.

I watched him take himself in at an impossible angle so that anyone else would have been sure that the wheels were going to smash him. The Blue Jay was a beat behind him, and for a moment, I was sure he would be too late to break Carrunner's concentration. He was a full yard away when Carrunner came to the point of no return. I watched him graze his whiskers against the turning wheel and then pull away all in one smooth motion. I felt his exhilaration. It was like the trucks had passed without crushing me and I had made it! I rejoiced in his triumph. I should have known better.

Just as Carrunner made his break and started on his outward course, riding the tangent that would carry him out of danger, the Blue Jay flashed alongside his face only a foot off the ground and rapped him above the right ear. It was all that was necessary. I started to scream against it because I could see his concentration decaying, and I knew what was going to happen next.

It all came rushing back, that indescribable elation, that

incredible sense of mastery, and then, when I was about to swing back into the right lane in front of the truck, the push from the truck I was passing dropped off to nothing and the backwash of the passing truck hit me from the left and knocked the bike out from under me. The handlebars were attached to the horizon and I tried to lift the planet up and to the left. The horn was a buzzing that filled up the world. I saw Carrunner lean the same way, jerked out of his path and back under the car.

He went into a narrow, flat space between the dark undercarriage of the car and the cement of the road. He went in behind the front wheels, and he must have known there was nothing for him to do but keep going. Then the hump of the transmission hit him and slammed him down into the street. He bounced back up, and the car hit him again and dribbled him out the other side. I could feel him going down, the bike shooting out from under me, and the cement coming up like an explosion. I could feel myself bouncing with him, and then flipping over like a limp rag being blown out of the way of the rushing backwash of the truck.

He went cartwheeling out on the other side of the car, but the rear wheel caught his tail and flung him down again. Everything seemed to be grating. The brakes of the car were metal on metal like the sound of my bike grinding under the front bumper of the truck. Everything went pinwheeling, impact after impact, like being taken by the foot and slammed down, stiff as a ruler, again and again. I thought he was dead. I thought I was dead.

But he kept going out the other side and kept on running up the curb and under a parked car in someone's driveway. And only when he had gotten there did he cry out, all his pain breaking out of him in one long wail of torment, fear, and horror. I knew what he felt like lying there under that car, smelling the gasoline and feeling the crust of old oil stains against his face, waiting for someone to come along and take charge of things, thinking that it had finally happened, the most horrible thing you can imagine, and you are lying there dumbfounded in the face of the twin impossibilities that you are alive and that there is no pain. You wonder how there can be no pain when you know some of your bones have been shivered into sawdust, and your jeans are full of blood, and your foot is facing the wrong way, the wrong way!

I could see him shivering under that car, waiting for the pain he knew was coming, helpless and amazed. I looked away, followed the Blue Jay back over the houses to the lot, clinging to the sight of him and remembering when I rolled over that final time and everything settled into place, dull and fuzzy, through the fog of my numbness, I could see, sitting in a short pine tree greener than anything that could be imagined, sitting just behind a brush of long needles, the most beautiful thing I had ever seen—a blue jay staring at me out of that black mask he wore beneath his blue hood, staring at me with those black eyes down the sword of his beak. I could see him double, on the tree and on the curving plastic face mask of my helmet where he seemed to sit on the branches of the feathery cracks. I could never tell which one was real and which was the reflection.

Someone came and got Carrunner out from under the car. He should have been dead. I should have been dead. If someone had told me then that he would be walking down the street in six weeks, I would not have believed it. But there is apparently a special Providence that takes care of fools. It took better care of me than it did of Carrunner. My broken places healed, but Carrunner had no helmet, and when they brought him back from the veterinarian's, he was never the same.

His tail was gone, shortened to a stub, but his mind had been broken off much shorter. His head seemed to be shaped funny, and thereafter he was full of idiotic, unrelated motions, like all of his circuits had been reconnected by someone who had no experience with them and no schematic to follow.

He walked all right, but he would end up in strange places, and he had a dull expression as if he was still, and would always be, in shock. When the Blue-Haired Lady let him out of the house for the first time, he came down the steps like he had never been there before, and he was always coming into the wrong house and looking around like some cruel joke was being played on him by people who had repainted the kitchen and moved his dish around.

Wise Teacher was waiting for him when he came out. I believe Carrunner did not recognize him at first because he started to move away to the side as if he was afraid, but it may have been that he did not see very well and was continually being surprised that out of the fog of his vision something familiar would emerge.

Wise Teacher walked around him, cocking his head to see if it could truly be Carrunner so misshapen in his attitude, so distorted in his approach to the world. But in a few minutes, Wise Teacher had apparently satisfied himself that it was indeed Carrunner and that he was somehow responsible for him. After a few minutes of cat amenities, they went away side by side on their rounds, traveling next to each other in worlds so separate that it made the heart ache to see them.

Carrunner's Last Stand

Undoubtedly Wise Teacher was under no legal obligation
to do what he did. His contract with Carrunner had been
terminated weeks before. Carrunner had graduated in his
own way and had gone into business for himself. Past a
certain age, cats have no obligations of family. They don't
complain about having been brought into this world, and
they feel no obligation to those who brought them in.
Fatherhood has little meaning to them, and motherhood,
intense as it may be, is a short-lived biological necessity. A
kitten is everybody's responsibility; a cat is no one's worry
except its own.

Kittens become cats very quickly. Any mature cat will
advise them along the way, any grown cat will offer at least
grudging assistance to any other cat not yet mature enough
to be a threat. I doubt that Wise Teacher thought of

113

Carrunner as either a brother or a son, and yet his loyalty to him was far greater than to either.

If both he and Carrunner had been totally wild and had had no steady source of food, I do not know how long Wise Teacher would have been able to carry him, but even living as they did, it cost him a good deal just to put things back nearly as they had been. Perhaps he did it by thinking of Carrunner as a kitten. He would not have been far wrong, except that Carrunner seemed to have lost some things and gained others. He had in a sense ceased to be a cat in some ways, just as the Mad Squirrel had ceased to be a squirrel.

The bobbed tail made him look like a starved Manx cat, and his head no longer looked exactly Siamese. It was not entirely deformed, but it seemed lopsided and it made his eyes seem oddly shaped. The eyes were vacant a good part of the time. They were different from Wise Teacher's eyes. There was never a time when there was not something going on behind Wise Teacher's eyes, and Carrunner had been no different. But after he came back, he seemed to suffer from major short circuits, minor internal fires, and complete power failures.

He seemed bewildered most of the time. He always had a way of rubbing himself up against any human leg he found handy. It was probably a constant source of pleasure for both him and the Blue-Haired Lady who fed him. After the accident, he would rub the back of his head up against Wise Teacher, nudging the back of his ear against Wise Teacher's side or brushing his shoulder against Wise Teacher's chest. It was indecorous behavior at best, and if it had occurred earlier, no doubt Wise Teacher would have chastised him severely. But after the accident, he only seemed embarrassed by it and did not pull away. He stood perfectly still, staring off into space as if it were not happening until Carrunner was finished.

I doubt that Carrunner was even aware that he was

doing it. Sometimes he would rub his flanks along Wise Teacher and suddenly leap away from him with a cry that was somewhere between startled and outraged. I believe he could not distinguish between memory and reality most of the time. No doubt, in his mind, he was rubbing against the Blue-Haired Lady's leg, only to have it turn suddenly into Wise Teacher. When it happened, there was always a hint of bewildered terror in his cry, as if he had come to live in a nightmare where things kept changing into other things without warning; a leg would become Wise Teacher and a bush would suddenly become the Black Dog. He did not seem to understand how Wise Teacher could walk so obliviously through the madness of the new world. It did not seem to occur to him that only he had changed.

There was a period after he first came back when his behavior was always at odds with expectation. He would startle at everything that moved and leap out of the way of anything white. He would lunge away from any car he passed whether it was moving or parked, and he would flatten down if the shadow of a passing bird fell on him. He would stand sometimes with his front feet in his water dish and then suddenly leap away and then shake his feet off and look at the Blue-Haired Lady as if she had just played a nasty trick on him. She cried when she told me about that, and I believe Carrunner was a greater burden to her than to Wise Teacher. I saw it wear her away over the months.

More than once during the first week, Carrunner blundered in the direction of the Black Dog without seeing him. That was the most peculiar thing, that he seemed oblivious to the Black Dog after it had formed such a major part of his existence for so long. Carrunner had always had an absolute terror of the Black Dog, as did everything else with any sense, but his had been even more extreme than most.

I never saw him walk on the same side of the street as

the Black Dog's house, and the sound of a chain moving across the macadam would put him into instant flight. Even the Black Dog's bark would sometimes make him give out an involuntary howl, if he was close enough; and drowsing on the Blue-Haired Lady's lap, he would sometimes startle from a dream with his fur standing on end, uttering that same cry.

The only time he would voluntarily get within half a block of the Black Dog was when he stood beside the tree at the corner getting ready to defy death. In his less suicidal mind, he shunned the dog. If I saw him twitching in his sleep, stretched out in the backyard sun, I knew it was the Black Dog he was dreaming about. But when he came home from the vet's, he seemed not to know who the Black Dog was or even that he was there.

Twice in the first day, he walked resolutely toward the danger zone, bringing the Black Dog to his feet, and only Wise Teacher's continually getting in front of him made him change his direction before he got too close. He got worse before he got better, and for the first week he seemed to be going constantly in a fatal direction. It happened so often and his life had become so hard that I had an inkling that it might be suicide that drove him. But whatever it was, Wise Teacher's patient intervention turned him away from it again and again.

The third day he was home, he was almost to the edge of the macadam when it seemed to dawn on him that the black shadow flying toward him was the dog. The roar of the Black Dog was instantly drowned out by the most terrifying scream I can remember. His life must have been a child's nightmare. To be walking peacefully along and suddenly have the most ferocious monster of your dreams appear out of nowhere must have been pure horror. Wise Teacher watched him constantly after that. It cut into his duties enormously.

Watching Carrunner was a full-time job, and it distracted him from following his rounds. But Carrunner learned to adjust with his help, and they were always together. If some dream seemed real to him, Carrunner would look to Wise Teacher before he reacted. If a bush moved and Carrunner thought it was a dog or a demon, he looked to Wise Teacher for confirmation before raising his hackles. But I could see the terror shivering under his skin in that instant between when he saw whatever apparition had started his heart racing and the instant he looked to Wise Teacher for corroboration.

It must have kept Wise Teacher on edge, having to check every few minutes to see if there was a real threat at hand or just another Blue-Point hallucination. It was like having a fire alarm going off constantly in a place where a real fire is possible at any minute. Smaller dogs and a few medium size ones often slipped out doors left open momentarily and ran free for a few minutes until someone called them back. Wise Teacher was too prudent to ignore the warnings, and I never saw him fail to provide feline reassurance, even if it was only to look in the direction in question and remain unmoved.

But it made his rounds take twice as long, and it began to make him nervous. He would be poking at something mysterious in the lot or looking under a porch when Carrunner would startle and Wise Teacher would jerk his head back out and startle himself. About half the time, his sudden crouch would send Carrunner into a frenzy, shrieking and darting in a zigzag course back and forth across the lot until Wise Teacher could calm him down again.

Sometimes he would have to turn reluctantly away from some unusual puzzle entirely because Carrunner would rattle every time he poked his head under something. If Wise Teacher crawled under a car to get out of the sun or to sneak up on a bird, Carrunner howled continuously until he came out. Hunting was difficult at best. There was no telling when, after they had crawled up so silently on some half-witted starling, Carrunner would leap up in panic and set the quarry on the wing.

It was hard to decide which was worse, when he startled the prey or when he went crawling across the grass to pounce on a leaf the wind had stirred. He did not know where he was most of the time and he was constantly being fooled by instant replays in his damaged brain that seemed real as life.

I watched him sit in the middle of the street as if he was sitting in front of his dish, moving his head back and forth like he was looking up at the Blue-Haired Lady passing back and forth in front of him. Then he meowed softly and finally rubbed himself against some invisible leg only he could see, trying to get the attention of an old woman who wasn't there. Suddenly he froze in that half-crouch he would go into when he heard something that might be danger but had not been located yet, and he looked around from side to side frantically, as if the kitchen had suddenly vanished, leaving him transported without transition into the middle of the street. He gave a frantic howl as if the tricks were too much for him. It was full of the anguish and terror of the inexplicable.

He just crouched in the street for minutes, howling over and over like a cat trapped in a high place it sees no way down from. At the end of each cry, there was a little dying whine, as if he would do anything not to be tormented anymore but couldn't find out what he should do. Finally the Blue-Haired Lady came out and gathered him up and hugged him and smoothed his coat back down and held him up near her face and talked sweetly to him until he calmed down. But when he clung to her sweater and hung his head over her shoulder, I could see in his eyes the absolute terror that she was going to disappear and he would find himself hanging in midair in some place he could not remember coming to.

From time to time, he would come into my house through the open back door and look at me like I was a trespasser. Then he would look around the kitchen, confused at the lack of rightness to it. He seemed certain he was in the right place, but everything was wrong—the wrong color, the wrong shape, the wrong smell. I was clearly wrong. He would look at me pleadingly to change it all back to the way it should be.

When I could, I would hobble out to the kitchen and give him some milk or a ball of hamburger. Then he would start to rub against my cast and suddenly leap away from it because it was not the soft, warm leg he had expected. He looked at me sidelong, as if anyone with a fake leg could be responsible for the rest of the tricks. After that, he came into the kitchen at least once a week, but he never seemed to trust me fully, as if he hoped to catch me off guard some time and figure out how it was that I kept transporting him from place to place without his knowing.

Because so many of the truly inexplicable events in any domestic animal's life are the acts of people, I suppose it seemed likely to him that there was bound to be a human behind his misery. Maybe he thought I acted suspicious. Probably I did. He made me nervous. I couldn't look at him without seeing him disappear into that crawl space under the car. I couldn't look at his head without seeing that transmission dribble it on the ground or his tail without seeing the back tire of that car pinning it to the road as he leapt away, yanking him back and slamming him down.

And whenever I saw those things again, my legs would hurt and my elbow would begin to throb and that cold sweat would come over me that always comes when I hear the blast of an air horn or the crash of metal, or the roar of a bike followed by the squeal of brakes. Sometimes when I saw him up close like that, it made me shiver. I suppose that made him think I had something to do with the monstrous tricks that were incessantly being played on him.

Maybe he thought that by confronting me and showing me that he was harmless, I would stop tormenting him. Whenever I gave him something to eat, he would take it and then wait as if it was a token that I wasn't mad at him anymore and might lift the curse of illusion from him. But maybe it was only my own distortion of what was happening. Maybe he just wanted another ally, another human being to handle his case.

I gave him what I could, but there was really nothing much I could do for him. Wise Teacher was the only one who could help him, and from time to time, Wise Teacher would come into my kitchen as well and herd Carrunner out. It was always as if he had been looking everywhere for him to take him along on his rounds and had finally found him. Sometimes he would just look in through the angle of the open door and call to him impatiently. Invariably Carrunner went, whether he was finished or not.

I tried once to give Wise Teacher a ball of hamburger too, but he came close enough to see what it was and then turned his nose up at it and walked away as if I'd insulted him by offering him a handout. Carrunner went after him like a little brother tagging along, and it seemed to me that Wise Teacher only let him investigate things that had no importance but would keep him busy. Things went on like that and settled into a routine, but they did not get noticeably better.

After the first month, Carrunner had learned to keep his panics down to a minimum, but it was still obvious that he was only in the real world a diminishing portion of the time, and he seemed to lapse into brooding stillnesses more and more often. When the weather started to turn cold, he got worse, as if the cold made the bones of his head contract. I knew what he felt like; storms always started in my legs long before they marched across the sky, and cold seemed to seep through blankets, long underwear, and anything else as if it was not so much a matter of temperature as of season. Carrunner and I ached our way into winter together.

Whenever I looked at his suffering, my legs seemed trivial. He seemed to be in a lot of pain, and he would yowl for hours on end some nights. You could hear his voice even when he was in the Blue-Haired Lady's house, and when he was outside, he would suddenly burst into a fit of yowling as if he couldn't hold it in any longer. People began to talk to the Blue-Haired Lady about having him put to sleep, but she wouldn't hear of it anymore than the mother of a retarded child would listen to such nonsense. There was a lot of talk about actions "for his own good," but before any of it came to fruition, Carrunner took matters into his own hands.

I saw him the afternoon he went to settle his affairs. He came walking down the driveway slowly, almost like he was stalking something. He twisted his head toward his shoulder a couple of times as if his head hurt, and when he picked it up each time, his eyes were squinted shut. He looked as if he knew something was going to happen. When he got to the end of the driveway, he turned left and walked up to the south corner of the lawn and sat there.

It was an odd place for him to sit. Whenever I saw him, he was always in the backyard or in the driveway. I never saw him on the Blue-Haired Lady's property anyplace where the house was not between him and the Black Dog. But from where he sat, the Black Dog could see him fairly easily if it came to the middle of its chain. It got up from back near the garage and walked over to where it could see him better and laid down as if it was waiting for something.

I had that feeling of an event drawing itself together again, just as I had when Carrunner went to the wheels. I could see a straight line connecting them, but even though energy seemed to crackle over it like microwaves, the focus of everything did not seem to be there yet. But I had no idea what it was until I looked further down the street and saw the Orange Cat coming across the avenue, heading down toward the lake. Behind her were two young cats, a male and a female. They trotted behind her, looking around at everything. Both seemed almost grown, and I knew that within a week or two, they would be on their own.

They were downwind, and the Black Dog was staring too hard at Carrunner to notice them. I don't know what mental lapse could have made the Orange Cat walk along that sidewalk like a human being out for a stroll, unless it was some sort of final exam for the fittest of the litter. Nothing on four legs went on that side of the street by choice except the Little Dog with the Big Voice.

I felt everything start to grind forward like a train starting up. Carrunner must have seen them but he did not give it away. He just kept on washing himself, licking each paw slowly and thoughtfully and cocking his paw and looking at his claws like he wished they were longer. He must have known somehow what was going to happen. From time to time, he looked up and stared eye to eye at the dog.

I knew what he felt like looking at that dog—the way I felt when I saw a bike: like I wished I could get back on it but knew I never would. Everything seemed to tighten together again, and I could feel it like some huge vibration running up octave by octave toward a cosmic collision. It was like the motor of a bike being revved up, getting louder and stronger with every twist of the throttle until the Orange Cat came almost even with the Black Dog and everything snapped. It was like somebody had suddenly kicked the event into gear and it stood up on its back wheel and went screeching forward.

The Black Dog's huge head swung toward the street and

froze. The Orange Cat went right past and the female followed her, but the male stopped and looked straight in the Black Dog's face with a look that was part curiosity and part defiance. The dog seemed to leap at it without standing up, and there was a loud *ping* as the chain broke. The young cat shot forward, and the Black Dog scrambled after it like he was too hungry to think straight. His growl built to a snarl that could only end in a bite.

Even before Carrunner began, I could see where it was all going to intersect. He moved with the old grace, like he was catapulting himself toward the wheels again. The straight lines converged. The Black Dog's line ran parallel with the young cat's, but Carrunner's line intersected it at an angle of attack that allowed no veering away at the last moment.

There was a split second as he came to the boundary line of the Blue-Haired Lady's yard, half a length behind the young cat, when the Black Dog seemed to snap his head toward Carrunner and then back toward the fleeing youngster like he was trying to decide which he wanted more. But he must have thought Carrunner was only a decoy and he turned back to his original target without losing a step. It was a big mistake.

Carrunner crouched and sprang. He looked like a tiger in the air, and he hit the Black Dog along the side with all four feet. For a moment, he looked like he was trying to climb up the Black Dog's side and ride him. But the Black Dog lunged sideward and rolled his shoulders, and Carrunner started to slip free. One of his hands came loose, but he slammed it back into position like a dock walloper whacking a baling hook into a crate. The Black Dog howled.

The Orange Cat shot past my house and kept going. The young cats were only half a stride behind her. The dog snapped his head around in full flight, twisting himself against his forward momentum, and his jaws clamped shut on Carrunner. Then his head rolled forward again and Carrunner's claws worked like machines, raking the Black Dog's side in short ripping motions as he was pulled free.

The Black Dog skidded to a stop. He had Carrunner around the middle, and he shook him from side to side like a rat and flung him a good five feet up onto the lawn. Carrunner hit and rolled. He had not been as far back in the Black Dog's jaws as the Little Dog had, and he was blood from shoulder to hip. The Black Dog went for him as he was lying on his side, but Carrunner swiped at him and raked his nose.

He caught the scar tissue the Mad Squirrel had left, and it must have raked up old memories that made the Black Dog leap back. It was not enough to drive him away, but it seemed to trigger some reflex the Mad Squirrel had carved into him, and he hesitated. He was gathering himself for a second lunge when Howler came out onto the sidewalk and started yelling threats. The Black Dog wavered between revenge and obedience, but finally he turned away and put his tail between his legs and trotted back to his chain.

Howler came after him with a bamboo cane that was splintered halfway up so that it made a loud crack whenever it was snapped, whether it hit something or not. The Black Dog cringed and crawled and rolled over on his back in absolute surrender. Howler kept shouting at him and cursing him and menacing him with the cane. The Black Dog whined like a puppy, but Howler smacked him with the cane and pointed to the garage. The Black Dog slunk toward it, half-crawling, half-running as the cane rose and fell, rose and fell.

I doubt that the cane hurt him all that much; it was puppy memories that made him cringe, terrors that were put into him when he was still small and defenseless, fears that he never got rid of, and for a minute I felt sorry for the Black Dog and understood a little how he had become what he had become.

When I looked back for Carrunner, he was gone. I believe he had crawled into the bushes at the side of the house, because when the neighborhood tried to find him for the Blue-Haired Lady, he was nowhere around.

But a little after dark, I saw him come out of the tangle of forsythia at the side of the front porch. He was barely moving, but there seemed to be a little of his old strut in his walk. Wise Teacher appeared out of nowhere along the fence and trotted over to him. They talked for a moment, short, soft *miaaows*, like good-byes and thanks. Then Carrunner made one final sound full of peace and serenity that died away into silence.

Then he went slowly off down the street toward the lake, and I knew he was doing what cats do when they are going to die. He was going off alone to seek a private death. It was why Wise Teacher did not go with him. It was something he was entitled to.

It was getting dark quickly, and I lost him before he was halfway down the street, but I knew he was going down to the lake, and that's where they found him the next day, lying out in the middle of the ice where nobody could bother him. It was too thin to go out and get him, and when the ice broke up, he disappeared stiff-legged under the water like a burial at sea.

For the first time in months, my legs stopped hurting and my elbow and shoulders moved without a sharp stab of pain, and I wondered what Wise Teacher would do with his life without somebody to teach. Around midnight, he went across the street into the middle of the lot to the place where the Mad Squirrel had fallen out of the sky between him and Carrunner. The moon was half-full, and I could see him sitting where the frost was beginning to form on

the grass, like he was trying to understand it all. He sat
there for a long while, and when a cloud went across the
moon and no one could see him, he stretched back his head
and gave a long, sharp wail of grief and loneliness more
eloquent than speech.

The Lion Dog

The day before the Lion Dog came, a package arrived for the Old Retired Man. The mailman handed it to me by mistake. It was a soft, reinforced envelope with a bottle inside. I could feel some kind of liquid moving in it when I turned the envelope over in my hand. It addressed the Old Retired Man as "Doctor," which was a surprise to me. The return address was the New York zoo, but the name on it had neither a title nor even "mister" in front of it. All it had was a first and a last name, the way anyone might send a letter to an old friend.

The package had a funny smell to it, a little like ammonia but with a strong but undefinable undertone that made me vaguely nervous without reason. I really wanted to know what was in that bottle, but I restrained myself from opening it "by accident." Even the thought of it was a breach of propriety that would have appalled the Old Retired Man and his wife, although they would probably have accepted my lie at face value.

The Old Retired Man and I had a nodding acquaintance that consisted of pleasantries about the weather and each other's health. We had talked from time to time for a few minutes, but our life-styles were too different for us to have much in common. We had an aloof but mutual respect, the way creatures of different species might share a common boundary in peace and harmony and still not have much to bind them together.

They were creatures from another time, a dignified, quiet, responsible time before the wars, and I was something out of a faster, wilder, more chaotic time, when their world had disintegrated and nothing much had taken its place. They were Seal Points in mixed-breed times, or maybe it was just that they were the main thrust of the species and I was another twisted mutation like the Mad Squirrel. In any case, I gave the package back to the mailman and let go of it, except as a mystery.

I got my first clue to what was going on when the Old Retired Man took the Little Dog out for his walk. But I did not begin to figure it out until Wise Teacher came along, and it was not until I remembered that the Lhasa apso was called a Lion Dog that it really dawned on me.

There was no mistaking the significance of the Little Dog's walk. Watching Wise Teacher had taught me that when a creature disrupts its routine, something significant is going on, and when the distruption amounts to an almost complete reversal of a pattern, something very important is happening. The Old Retired Man had always walked the Little Dog a little after midnight, except on Fridays, when the "Wild Kingdom" reruns were on the local syndication channel. Then he waited until twelve-thirty.

He was a little hard of hearing, and I could sometimes

hear the sound of the program through the window. I think the longest conversation we ever had was about the animals of the neighborhood and how we both watched them. He never said what job they had retired him from, but I got the impression that it had had to do with animals and research in some way, and that his interest in them was professional as well as a hobby.

Even where our interests overlapped, our motivations were different. I'm nocturnal as a cat anyway, but some nights, there was nothing inside to think about but pain, and I used to look out my front window all night long to get my mind off what there was no changing. Sometimes the cats would go by and I would watch them for a while, and then I'd watch the way the shape of things changed as it got lighter and the way the colors of the sky changed as the sun came up.

When the Old Retired Man hadn't come out by two, I began to wonder if he was sick, but around four A.M., he came out with the Little Dog, and they went north toward the lake end of the street. I thought it was a peculiar time for him to be out walking the dog, but it was too early for the cats and too late for the dogs, and it was the perfect time if he wanted to do something unobserved. And he apparently did, because everywhere the Little Dog stopped to mark his passage, the Old Retired Man bent over and did something to the tree. I couldn't tell what he was doing until they were coming back from the opposite direction on the far side of the street, and then I noticed that he was carrying an old shampoo bottle with a pump spray, and he was spraying something just above the Little Dog's mark.

I did not put it together with the bottle from the zoo until an hour or so later, when Wise Teacher came along. He came trotting down my driveway, and when he hit the wall of odor as he passed the last tree the Old Retired Man had sprayed, he did a sideways leap without breaking stride. His body froze there for a minute and then it went slack, the way someone who hears a noise lets himself relax when he finds out for sure that the "burglar" is only a scraping branch.

He looked up at the tree and made one of those sounds people who own cats use to convince themselves that cats are almost human instead of the other way around. That odor must have hit him with the force of legend, a cat so big it could devour a dog like a mouse, the Great Clawmother. It was probably as close as Wise Teacher could come to the concept of a god, an ancient memory of what the ancestors who lived in his genes were like. It was probably why he knew the identity of that smell, while the dogs did not.

He walked over to the tree one foot at a time, with that swing-raise-swing-place-settle kind of walk that meant he was going into a dangerous mystery and wanted to be sure where each foot was before he moved the next and unbalanced himself. He was making sure not to be caught leaning into something fatal. It took him longer to go the last five feet to the tree than it took to stalk a robin. Each foot came down where another foot had just left, and when he had walked his own footsteps to the bottom of the tree, he made a half-circle around it, keeping on the sidewalk side. He spotted the wet slash just up from the base, and he stretched up and got his nose and his eyes so close to it that his whiskers were bending back. Then he pulled back and looked around the tree. Nothing else was different. It was the only thing that had changed since he went by before, and nothing that strong could have gone by and not left a trace. I think he saw the Old Retired Man's hand in it right from the start.

But it wasn't until the Black Dog went by that I began to understand what was happening. The fur on the back of the Black Dog's neck went up when he was still half a block away, and the closer he got to the tree, the more his teeth showed and his ears flattened. When he got to the tree, he was growling without knowing why. There was no way he could have known what had made that mark, but something in his genes told him that what he was smelling was Alien Death.

But the smell was only half of it. The real problem was the vertical line. For a dog, the line he signs the tree with leaves a wealth of information for the nose that follows him. It will tell his diet, his sleeping habits, his state of mind. Even if it's only a stain that can hardly be seen, it will tell how big, how strong, how vigorous, and how aggressive the dog was. Put simply, the biggest dog leaves the highest vertical line because he can lift his leg higher.

Exactly how high the line runs tells the height of the dog. What tells his vigor is the verticality of the line, its strength; whether it trails off in a rising arc or whether it turns back down on itself as it would with an old dog or a sick one for whom standing on three legs is painful and difficult for any length of time. The Black Dog measured the tree with his nose, from its roots upward. Information was available to him in sheets of expanding and thinning odor that formed the dissipating scent. The concentration of the scent should be thinner as it goes up, as evaporation causes it to rise and spread out. How steep the gradient from bottom to top tells how long the natural rising process has been at work on it, how long since the mark was made.

Howler tried to pull him away from the tree, but it was a useless effort. The scent stirred something in the programs left by the Black Dog's ancestors that told him that Four-legged Death itself had marked the tree. There was another odor right next to it, and it took him a few minutes to sort them out; but when he did, the information made him even more angry than he was afraid. The other mark belonged to the Little Dog. The Black Dog went down the street alternately snarling and giving a worried growl, and by the time they came back up the same way, he was straining at the leash to get back to the safety of his chain.

Thereafter, every morning around four, the Old Retired Man would come out with the Little Dog and his lion spray, and every night the Black Dog would hit that smell and his ears would go back and down. But frightening as that scent was, it did not become truly terrifying until it began, day by day, to rise up the tree. There were only two kinds of dog whose mark rises up the tree from day to day—a dog recovering from a wound and one that is growing.

The Old Retired Man had made the first mark at the level of the Black Dog's nose, so he could not miss it. That made the new dog at least as big as the Black Dog to begin with. The quality of the scent was horror enough, but the fact that it was growing was a death sentence. The consequences were obvious. The Lion Dog was growing, and as it grew, so would its territory. The Old Retired Man made sure of that as well. Every day he raised the Lion Dog's marker a shade higher than the day before, and every day he extended its territory a little further.

At first, the claims to territory spread north toward the lake. But after a couple of weeks, they turned gradually east where the lake curved around and finally continued south across the avenue until the territory of the Lion Dog surrounded the Black Dog like a half-moon. East of the Black Dog, down the avenue toward where the bridge went over the lake to the next town, it was saturated. When Howler put the Black Dog on his leash and tried to take him down the avenue, he had to pull and curse and kick at the Black Dog until he got tired and let him go down the street toward the lake.

Every night the Black Dog would go by the tree in front of the Old Retired Man's house, and the line would rise a little higher above the Little Dog's signature, and every night he got quieter and quieter and his crouch got lower and lower until he went by that tree in a running crawl with his ears flat back along his head and his tail between his legs. Whenever he came to a new mark, he would go up to it and investigate it even though he could tell from ten feet away whose mark it was.

Down by the lake, the Old Retired Man would only spray every other day, so the scent was dilute enough to make the Black Dog come closer to it. At first, he would stretch his neck up to get all the information he could from it. The closer he got, the more the hackles on his neck would go up and the longer they would take to come down again.

As the mark moved gradually higher and higher up the tree near the lake, the Black Dog put first one foot and then the other up on the trunk until eventually the Old Retired Man had him standing on his hind legs. The Old Retired Man was patient in his war of nerves. Slowly he moved the line around the trunk as well as up it until he had the Black Dog dancing in terror around the tree on his hind legs, trying to follow the erratic pattern his nose told him was there.

The tree by the lake was the only place where the scent was light enough for the Black Dog to stand it. The scent of the Lion Dog steadily closing in on him from three sides frightened him, but it did not worry him as much as the fact that the Little Dog's scent mark was always right there with it.

The significance was inescapable; they marked the same territory, which meant that either they were equals or, at the very least, that the Little Dog was under the protection of the Lion Dog, like a puppy. But there were a lot of things that did not make sense, and it was the contradictions that really frightened him. There was no telling what he was dealing with. The Lion Dog's scent was not what it should be. It was not entirely the mark of a dog, nor was it entirely like a cat. And yet it had all the traits of a dog, and it was in the company of a dog, so it had to be a dog.

Whatever it was, his nose told him that it not only ate

meat but ate it raw and bloody, not the processed meat
that some human being spooned out of a can but meat that
was either still alive or recently killed. It had the kind of
traces he found when the Free Dogs came by and left a
note of disrespect along the avenue for any of the tame dogs
who happened by. Sometimes during the fall, when the
remnants of deer season were left in plastic bags to be
taken away by the garbage men, one or another of the tame
dogs would leave a changed scent that said it was eating
blood and muscle. But the Lion Dog ate nothing else, and
it staggered the Black Dog's mind whenever he thought of
how big and meaty a creature would have to be to feed that
growing appetite.

There was another oddity: the Little Dog's mark was
always a little more tenuous, had spread itself on the rising
air currents of the day a little more than the scent of the
Lion Dog. It meant that the Little Dog did not follow along
like a puppy whose marking of his protector's trees was
tolerated. It meant that he was either the Lion Dog's
superior or had some control over him that made the Lion
Dog do him the deference of waiting until the Little Dog
had marked the territory first. In any case, it made
retribution inevitable.

If it were simply a question of the Lion Dog challenging
him for mastery of the territory, the Black Dog might roll
on his back and do deference, he might beg and whine and
be allowed to surrender his claims and remain unharmed.
But the Little Dog carried scars the Black Dog had put
there, and for that, there was only one kind of retribution.
There was no backing away from their vengeance. When
the smallest of the Free Dogs had come onto his territory,
he had let it alone because he knew that the leader of the
pack is responsible for those under him. If he had attacked
the scout dog, he would have had to reckon with the leader
of the Free Dogs, under whose protection all dogs in the
pack traveled.

There was no mistaking it. If the Little Dog was under the protection of the Lion Dog, the Black Dog had violated that protection the day he had mutilated the Little Dog, and he would have to pay for it. If the Lion Dog, for some unfathomable reason, was a follower of the Little Dog instead, he could legitimately be sent to administer the Little Dog's justice. The only thing that was difficult to understand was why it had not already happened. The worry grew daily. The delay was no consolation for him; the longer it was put off, the more terrible would be the final reckoning.

He must have come to the conclusion that the Lion Dog was waiting until it was fully grown before it paid off the debts of honor still outstanding. The thought of that coming confrontation must have begun to weigh on the Black Dog, because he barked less often and never answered the challenges of the Little Dog. Even his warnings to the other dogs, who began to gradually encroach on his territory, grew more feeble and more infrequent, until the least adventurous of them were signing their passage almost at the edge of the macadam.

The tame dogs walked the same route the Lion Dog walked, and they knew as well as the Black Dog that there was a new top dog who had done everything but put the old one in his place. They still did the Black Dog the deference the third most important dog in the territory deserved, and no one was about to challenge him, but it was a fact of life that there was a presence in the neighborhood that made the Black Dog a pipsqueak. They could read the air as well as the Black Dog, and they knew how things stood. They waited for the inevitable confrontation with anxious enthusiasm as the Lion Dog grew.

Finally, when it was well above the head of even the Black Dog standing on his hind legs, the line stopped moving higher. From then on, it only got thicker and stronger. The Black Dog began to fidget, waiting for the inevitable. The Old Retired Man let things level off for a few days, and then he began to take the Little Dog out for its walk five minutes earlier every day. The time difference was as obvious to the Black Dog as a neon sign. The first night he recognized it, he let out a howl and then cut it off in mid-syllable as if he was afraid the Lion Dog was listening. He turned away from the first tree he came to and slunk back toward his chain.

Every night, the Old Retired Man came out five minutes sooner, and every few nights, he moved the thickest mark closer and closer to the Black Dog's domain. The Black Dog even stopped barking at the mailman and just lay on his strip of macadam waiting for the end. The scent of the Lion Dog came at him from everywhere. It rolled in like fog from further down the avenue. It was thick as smoke down the street. Even south of the avenue, it was so thick that he always looked apprehensively toward it, as if he expected the Lion Dog to emerge out of it at any moment like some huge, vague shape suddenly emerging from the fog.

There was only one place where the scent did not wall him in, and that was directly up the avenue to the west. When Howler tried to pull him in any direction but straight up the avenue, he would cringe and whine, and when Howler cursed at him and kicked him, he would only crawl and whimper. Howler complained to whoever would listen that the goddamned dog had become neurotic and he was thinking of having it put away and replacing it with a younger, meaner dog. He swore the damn thing would only walk along the avenue, straight as an arrow all the way to the superhighway, where it would sit and listen to the howling of the wild dogs from the town dump beyond the trees.

Nothing could make the Black Dog stray right or left from the avenue. He would not cross the street; he would only go straight ahead up the narrow corridor the Old

Retired Man had left him. The only time he was anything like himself was when he was up at the superhighway, straining toward the trees on the far side. When he was at home, he only lay silently on the macadam with his head between his paws, waiting for the end. He never got up without looking around first—not merely around, but *up* and around, as if he expected some giant foot to come crashing down between the trees and some impossibly huge head to push down through the leaves of the highest oak and pick him up and shake him like a rat.

I suspect that the Little Dog told him as much every time he came out, because his coming-out speech no longer ended with the joyous cry of a dog on the trail of a squirrel; it stopped with a loud growl that he always accompanied with a rapid shaking of the head, as if he had a rat in his mouth and was shaking it to death. Every night the Little Dog came out, his cry would say, "This is the night!"

Every time he heard it, the Black Dog would begin yelping and would not stop until Howler brought him into the house. Every night, the yelping began five minutes earlier. When there was less than half an hour between the Little Dog's walk and that of the Black Dog, he would begin to whine frantically to be brought in and would not go out again until after noon. He was like a condemned murderer waiting for execution, getting stay after stay and going to pieces more with each one. Finally it came.

Howler went out for the night and left him chained. When it was almost time for the Lion Dog to come out and mark his territory, the Black Dog jerked against the chain and whined and pleaded to be let loose. But Howler was not around, and when the time came, the Black Dog went suddenly silent and tried to hide himself under the bushes along the fence, where he crouched, whimpering softly. The neighborhood was quiet as death when the Old Retired Man opened his door. Even the Little Dog did not make a sound. Far away, the Free Dogs were baying after something in the night. They must have sounded tame and ordinary to the Black Dog as he waited to be devoured.

The Old Retired Man came slowly up the street with the Little Dog on his leash, and when they came to the macadam, they turned left and slowly walked up it. The Black Dog could smell them coming. I could almost smell them myself, and I knew the Old Retired Man had drenched the Little Dog with his sprayer. When the Little Dog got about a yard away from him, the Black Dog began to whine and roll on the ground. He looked like a bitch in heat, pleading that anything be done to him but violence. Then he got up and came very tentatively over to the Little Dog, rolled over and exposed his throat, begging for his life.

The Little Dog stood over him making up his mind. He had the mark of the Lion Dog on him, and the Black Dog would not have retaliated no matter what he did. I expected the Little Dog to take him by the throat and kill him where he lay, but there is a command the species puts into each of its members that forbids the killing of a supplicant. Instead, the Little Dog only looked at him with disdain, while the Old Retired Man reached down and unhooked the chain from the Black Dog's collar. The Black Dog licked his hand as he did.

When the collar was free, the Little Dog growled and the Black Dog was up and running. The Little Dog went after him with something between a growl and a roar to speed him on his way. He only chased him to the corner before the Old Retired Man whistled him back, and he came trotting with his head up as if he knew even better than the Old Retired Man what had transpired. The Black Dog was yelping his way up the avenue, and his voice trailed away toward the superhighway. The traffic was not very thick that late at night, and the odds were very good that he would get across.

The Old Retired Man stood for a moment listening to

the yelping die away in the distance. He looked as if he was wishing the Black Dog good luck. He waited patiently for the Little Dog to put his unmistakable mark on the house and the garage, the macadam, and the Black Dog's chain; then he picked up the Little Dog's leash and they went on their way back around the block and down toward the lake.

The mark of the Lion Dog disappeared after that, but from time to time, when the barking of the other dogs threatened to drown him out, the Little Dog with the Big Voice would give the cry of a dog in pursuit of a squirrel and let it die away into the growl of a very big dog shaking something like a rat, just to let them know who had been left in charge.

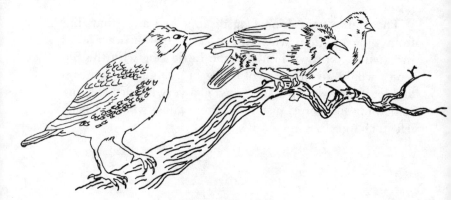

Winged Victory

The Blue Jay despised the starlings. He considered them riffraff and was continually in the process of evicting them, with greater and lesser success. He encountered least success in the winter. In the winter, the starlings traveled in gangs of twenty to a hundred birds, and attacking one of them caused the attacker to be mobbed by the entire flock. They were his outlaw bikers—loud, greedy, nasty, rowdy birds who looked disreputably disheveled at their worst and tastelessly dressed at best.

They had the bodies of second-rate crows and coats that bordered on the ridiculous. They were covered with white spots, like the victims of some loathsome communicable disease. The Blue Jay treated them as if they had painted the spots themselves to flout his authority. In winter, they were dirt brown to black under the spots, and some of them had green vests that looked like the oil rainbows that come naturally to a sloppy biker's denim vest.

Their feathers fluffed out like totally unkempt beards, and they had bellies that puffed out over a lot of sinewy muscle. They were a rough crew at best, especially in winter. The rest of the year, they were only pests. But in winter, food becomes scarce, especially for the single starling who is not so much a fighter as a loudmouth nobody wants to try.

The best a single starling can muster is usually a Mexican standoff, both sides glaring at each other and clenching and unclenching their fists, but nobody daring to throw the first punch; cowards trading insults until they can beat some kind of workable retreat. In the winter, they form up in gangs and forage in all directions until one of them spots something edible on the ground. There are a number of people on the property who will throw out bread and seed without a thought to whom it might encourage. It exasperates the Blue Jay, but the best he can do about it is try to drive the riffraff off until the legitimate tenants get their fill. But it's not easy; the starlings are organized.

Scouts fly a prearranged distance in an assigned direction and cry out when they find something. The successful forager is entitled to a finder's fee and sets up on the nearest safe perch. Others in the gang come in smaller numbers and take perches both higher and lower than the finder. The first ten form the clearing crew. Their cries attract the rest of the flock. When they are all in place, the first starling leaves the finder's perch and strafes the food without actually touching it. He flies back to a higher branch than before and immediately as he goes by, a starling on a lower branch shoots back along his trail and curves up, drawing off the attention of any pursuers. The third starling comes in on the food from the opposite side of the finder and may even touch down for a moment.

The finder then goes in on the first bread chunk and

back-wings clumsily over it, stretching out skinny, warty feet toward it but never quite grasping it. The Blue Jay is embarrassed for them every time they land. Sitting on a branch with their ugly feet tucked under them, they are excusable; but landing, they are an affront. Ducks can back-wing with style, swans can do it with grace; even vultures look, at worst, humorous. But the starlings are ugly; they make clumsiness a crime against the good name of birds. As far as the Blue Jay is concerned, the starlings are flying lizards.

The finder tries to hover over the food, but it is an awkward, ungainly, and finally untenable maneuver, and he has to flail his way back to the lowest perch like an inept swimmer. The clearing crew has a very precise order of attack, chancing the dangerous territory in small bits, one at a time, and with each one covering the escape route of the one preceding it. The rest of the flock takes the higher perches as the clearing crew makes the area secure. Usually they come in like a vertical sheet and seem to stick to the tree all over like a coating of flung pitch.

The member of the clearing crew who claims the second portion lands on the ground in the middle of the chunks of bread. But he does not eat. He walks around with his hands behind his back as if he is just looking over the property with the thought of investing in it. If nothing darts out and eats him, the finder lands and takes the first piece. If nothing leaps out and kills the both of them, the first lander takes his or her portion. The rest of the clearing crew lands in a flurry and takes a piece apiece. Sometimes they peck at several, as if testing them for taste or weighing them. They *walk* around, which is one reason the Blue Jay despises them. Any decent bird *hops*. Only lizards walk with that splay-toed step, that mechanical lifting of the leg with the foot flopping and then splaying out. It drives the Blue Jay to fury.

The starlings walk around the pieces, pecking at them

and analyzing them for difficulty of transport. The first to land usually take the smaller, more manageable pieces, since the territory being looted has not been proved entirely safe and fear is a stronger motivation to a starling than hunger. There are a lot of creatures that do not like starlings, and most of them are smart enough to wait until the entire flock is on the ground, where there is a better chance of catching one with its head down.

The Little Dog with the Big Voice harasses them continually, and Wise Teacher functions as the Blue Jay's gamekeeper, killing them just to keep their numbers down. A certain number of them are bearable, but they have a tendency to overstep themselves entirely, and Wise Teacher picks off the slowest or the slowest witted. To do so, he waits until the entire flock has landed and greed has taken the place of order.

He will watch them from a covert spot for minutes, waiting for some sacred proportion of them to have their heads down at the same time, and then he springs into their midst. Sometimes he has to go up on his hind legs to rake them down as they try to hop into the air, but whenever their number is excessive, he always brings down at least one. It's a hard job, but it serves a useful purpose. The other starlings are made wiser by his efforts, fitter to survive, more likely to live out the winter and reproduce hardier offspring.

In the winter, the Blue Jay has to take a lot from the starlings. Courageous as he is, the Blue Jay is no fool. He would like to dive into the biggest flock he can find and dispense justice, but it would be suicide. No doubt he would get the strike he went in for and would render one starling painfully aware of his wrath, but the rest of the flock would fold up on him like a closing fist and peck him to death before he could do a worthwhile amount of damage.

Usually the closest he comes is to take a higher perch

fifty feet away and curse them out. He has a range of notes in that turning-screw, metal-on-metal whistle of his, and he uses all of them to tell the starlings what he thinks of them. They ignore him. When the bread is gone, half of them continue to tramp around on the ground, looking for more with a kind of cranky desperation. Each starling in the flock has to decide when it is safe enough to go down on the ground and how long he or she can afford to wait before there isn't anything left worth going down for. Those whose cowardice exceeds their hunger come down too late for anything and stomp around on the ground, raising hell because nobody left them anything.

The Blue Jay hates them for that as well. They know the rules as well as he does. Those who take prudent risks prevail; those who are afraid to take risks or insist on taking foolish ones pay the price. The last ones down have nothing to complain about; they do not have sufficient courage to breed, and their cowardice justifiably dooms them to become the nonreproducing victims of the winter. They are afraid to take the risks, and as a result they will starve.

Sometimes even a finder will think the territory is too dangerous and will pass up his turn to take a common portion like the rest of the flock, who cascade down out of the tree all at once after the clearing crew has made sure everything is reasonably safe. If it were up to the Blue Jay, they would all perish. When he sits close to them, distracting them with that head-rattling scrape of his, Wise Teacher is usually around somewhere, sneaking up on them and waiting for the Blue Jay to break their concentration with his indignant accusations.

He is a lot happier in the summer. When food becomes more plentiful, fewer starlings need to be sent out before it is successfully found. Simultaneous finds by a number of starlings tend to splinter the flock into dozens of clearing crews. By summer, food is so plentiful that one bird acting alone has a good chance of finding enough to survive. The Blue Jay begins to get his revenge when the number of any clearing crew drops below six.

Five birds can't cover all the escape routes successfully; they are in danger of leaving him an opening right or left, front or back, up or down. They have to close in on him like a box—four sides, a lid, and a bottom—and smother him. More than six get in their own way usually, but if they form up correctly, they can get him and he knows it. He lives with that fact until the abundance of food shrinks the clearing crews below the number they need to retaliate. Then he tries to drive them out. He did it every year; it was one of those endless and insurmountable tasks that can only be kept abreast of. All winter he would fall behind; in spring and summer, he would catch up again, and in fall and winter, it would get gradually out of hand again.

At their peak, they would flout his authority openly, and all he could do was threaten them at a distance. When the odds evened up a little, he took his revenge with alacrity. But things were different after the death of his wife and the destruction of his line. The starling population went way up while he was imposing his justice on the squirrels and the cats, but he hardly seemed to notice. I could see the memories were wearing on him, taking their daily toll. Little hesitations began to creep into his rounds day by day, beginning with the gradually widening berth he gave the nesting tree and the hedge. I believe he could not fly over either of them from certain angles without seeing his wife flopping on the ground with that broken wing while Carrunner tortured her.

From certain positions in his flight, two objects would come into view like the triangulations he used to recover his seeds, and the memories would suddenly unearth like buried acorns. He could not go near the nesting tree without seeing the Mad Squirrel shredding the eggs that should have been the Blue Jay sons he could have trained to take over the property. He had had so much to pass on, and all he had left was obligations.

One by one, dozens of other spots seemed to affect him the same way; they bulged and distorted his route through the property until it was almost as erratic as a starling's. I do not believe I saw him anything but doggedly bitter after the Mad Squirrel tore his world down. None of his revenges helped. Not the death of the Mad Squirrel, nor the chastening of Wise Teacher, nor the terrible destruction of Carrunner gave him any comfort. They passed like obligations met. The property had become a ruin to him, and it was clear long before he finally did it that he was just waiting for someone worthwhile to pass it all on to, somebody who could hold it properly in the name of all blue jays.

Step by step, he had put the property in order so that it could be passed on to a successor. He had beaten the tenants into line sufficiently so it would not degenerate totally before the new jay could make his own reputation. And eventually there came a time, toward the end of winter, when the only loose end that remained was the starlings.

He had administered a harsh justice and restored a respect for properly constituted authority. He had re-established the power of his species to oversee its domain without attack. Having killed a member of royalty, the lesser nobles had been punished and the peasants had been taught to keep their place in the hierarchy, at the top of which a blue jay would always perch as steward of the land. There was little left to do.

February is the bottom of the year in New Jersey, the low point from which everything that survives into April rises. The weather is usually still cold and will turn drizzly for weeks before it becomes fair again. If the sun is out, it is bound to be below freezing. It is a time of deepest depression; everything seems to stagnate, to fall under a somber pall that says spring will never come and only a fool would wait for it. The Blue Jay seemed to feel it more keenly than anyone.

He spent more and more time in the higher air, up at the invisible roof of the property, and less and less in the lower branches and rain gutters. The usual levels of his daily inspection of the property narrowed. Instead of watching close to the ground, then higher up in the branches, and finally from above the trees, he spent more and more time aloft. It must have given him a more philosophic view of things, and like most philosophy, it turned first to introspection and then to melancholy.

The bustle went out of his flight. He did not follow his usual brisk routine from station to station, from lower branch to roof corner to higher branch to sky. He seemed to have removed himself, to have passed beyond any personal involvement in the affairs of the property. It was as if he had assured himself that things were in proper order and was almost ready to relinquish them to the next jay.

But it seemed like more than that—as if everything he saw from that high moving post made him think of what had happened there, his own personal loss, and his failure to defend against it. His efforts against the cats and his harsh reminder to the squirrels had set things in order again, but the fact remained that under his supervision, a tragedy had occurred, one which left him unfit to rule.

He stayed aloft longer and longer as the year went toward its lowest point, as if flying off the grief he had focused into vengeance. With the work done, there was too much time left for reflection, too much time to think of what could have been avoided if he had confronted the Mad Squirrel sooner or spent less time around the property and more around the nest. The "if onlys" sent

him aloft, and the "should haves" kept him there. With the
year bottoming out, it would be a good time to put the
place up for sale.

The spring would bring other jays, as it always did, but
he would not be there to show them through his domain,
allowing the regularity of its daily running to convince
them that it was in more capable hands than they could
offer. When the unlanded aristocracy came by in March
and April, he would not be there to offer them temporary
hospitality and send them on their way looking for less
capably managed realms to confiscate.

They would find a well-run, orderly house that a strong
jay could keep in order. The marks of what had happened
would be clear for any jay worthy of being his successor.
He had left intact the essentials. The way the tenants
treated the new jay would tell him that a terrible thing had
occurred and a terrible price had been exacted for it.

Several jays were bound to come, a few perennials who
came by each year to see if he had fallen victim to some
predator or had lost his touch, hoping to succeed where he
had failed. This time they would find the vacancy they had
always looked for. He had his favorites among the preten-
ders, but he would not stay to select a successor. The
tragedy had deprived him of that right. If he had felt
himself failing, if he had come to the end of his powers, the
end of his endurance, and was about to move to easier
property further south, he could have legitimately stayed
and held off applicants until the right one came along.
Then, after a few weeks of breaking in the new landlord, he
would have given up the property, with the proper
warnings and admonitions.

But he had no claim to either privilege or ceremony. He
had no rights left, only obligations, and all but one of those
was fulfilled. It was just the right time to leave—close
enough to spring for new jays to be already on their way,
long enough for the applicants to sort themselves out a

rightful successor, but not so long that whoever took over could sit idly by and let things deteriorate any further. Only the problem of the starlings remained.

The Blue Jay knew there would always be starlings in the lot, loud, raucous, uncouth. He hated them for their noisiness, for their commonness, their lack of discipline. But he hated them most for their addictions. Starlings were a bad lot at best, but the worst of them were anters and smoke-bathers.

It was true there were jays who anted, who plopped themselves down on anthills and spread their wings and let the vermin crawl all over them under the excuse that it was only medicinal, a necessary evil for the cure of parasites. He had even heard jays wax lyrical about the tingling, the indescribable sensation created by that net of motion. He had heard them sing about the whole body acrawl with sensation.

Once a visiting jay had perched in the backyard, picking up ants one at a time, rubbing them under his wing, three times on the left, once on the right, and gobbling them down when he had squeezed them dry. It was the only time I saw the Blue Jay treat a guest roughly. He danced back and forth on the rain gutter as if he wanted to dive in on the felon like it was a starling, but he restrained himself and only administered a scathing lecture about a jay's obligation to his kind and keeping up the image of the species. But the lecture did no good. The visitor was a young jay and was clearly addicted. When he found the youngster squirming down on another anthill the next day, the Blue Jay buzzed him. It was a warning to get out and never come back.

It was the debilitating sensuality he minded; the long-term effects that infuriated him. Addiction took away the will to work, the responsibility for the property. He had seen other jays become anters, had seen them spend more and more time on the anthills, less and less taking care of

business until their property went to chaos and bank-
ruptcy.

That kind of frivolity was a one-way process that led
always to the loss of the property and eventually to the loss
of life itself. A bird, any bird, sitting on the ground like that
with its eyes pulled closed, all ajingle with the feelings and
paying no attention to anything but the delicate web of
sensation the coat of ants produced, was doomed from the
first. A bird who spent that much time on the ground was
bound to become somebody's meal. And whoever took over
the property would have an impossible time reestablishing
any respect for jays as a whole.

A jay was better off avoiding the temptation entirely.
Few were strong enough to overcome it. The idea filled him
with an innate disgust. His version of the species was
meant for hard times; he had a preoccupation with
establishing order that bordered on compulsion. It did not
seem to occur to him that the tendency to ant was only a
mechanism for weeding out the unfit, so that only the most
dedicated would rule a piece of property. In the long run,
abstainers like himself would determine the outcome of the
species, while the rest justifiably died off. It bothered him
that of all birds, there could be jays so prone to debauch, so
weak in their commitment to the obligations of the species.

In starlings, the addiction could be expected if not
condoned, and if only a few of them had been anters, he
might have tolerated it. But the whole gang of them were
flagrant addicts. It was the outrageousness of their addiction, the way they flaunted it, that drove him to distraction. There was not a starling around who would not come
back again and again to the same anthill and satiate itself
over and over. Sometimes he would see a dozen in different
places on the property, taking their necessary dose anywhere there were insects. At night, when they went to the
tops of the trees and jabbered away until the whole flock
was in, it was all they talked about. He had heard their

cries of delight often enough on the anthills to know what they were talking about, to hear them comparing experiences, reliving them, mimicking their gestures in the throes of that ecstasy. The trees would rattle with their exuberant comparisons.

It was all ants—where they could be gotten, where they were thickest, what dangers one or the other of them had braved to get the best and the longest fix, how much they needed it, how they reveled in the sensation. Any one of them mimicking how he had picked up one juicy specimen after another and rubbed himself with it would set them all nodding and preening, rubbing imaginary insects along the delicate, sensitive wing feathers.

It disgusted him. Junkie starlings were more than a blue jay could be expected to stand. And they were worse in winter, when ants were impossible to come by, and there was nothing for them to do but complain about the drought and smoke-bathe. It was hard to say which disgusted him more, the anting or the sight of them perched on the rims of chimneys, spreading their wings over the rising smoke, reveling in the substitute tingling the hot air gave as it rushed through their feathers. The sheer hedonism of it appalled him.

They were like outlaw bikers massed for a five-month debauch, stoked on every pharmaceutical known to man. Whenever he could catch one or two of them alone on a chimney, he would dive at them and drive them off. But far more often than not, there were whole flocks on the roof line, waiting their turn, bitching and complaining that whoever was on the chimney was taking too long, or running themselves crazy with anticipation, talking about the summer gone or the summer to come filled with the endless delirium of ants. Or grumbling that the tingle of the smoke was too little and longing for the warm, ant-filled days of summer.

A dive among them would send the whole flock up in

tight little bunches that threatened collision for the diver. Clumsy, awkward fliers, they were as likely to knock a good flier out of the air by accident just getting out of the way as they were to concentrate sufficiently for an attack. The thicker the flocks got, the more dangerous it was to buzz them, and they had gotten thicker and thicker all winter.

It is possible that he let them get that bad on purpose, that he welcomed the risk of death he had let mount. Maybe he did it as a test for himself, to see if he was really fit to go on living. He had left the starlings until last because they were the most dangerous of his tasks, the one he might not live to finish. They were always the biggest problem any landlord faced in winter.

They outforaged every other bird, massing into enormous gangs that defied him continually by poaching even on his own favorite feeding spots. If bread or other crumbs were dispersed when there was snow or when there was cold, the starlings took almost all of it, leaving only shreds too small for a sparrow to bother about. He hated them with a vehemence that was only partly professional. They represented everything he despised—cowardice, weakness, greed; they lacked everything he thought important— discipline, responsibility, courage, independence. They were gaudy, ugly, ungainly birds, tramps and vagabonds, a plague of bums.

He hated them most because they were gang birds. Even blue jays were not above gathering in a flock, but they always traveled in discrete trios or small multiples of the sacred number. Starlings traveled by the score, and at night, they would fill a tree like noisy, vulgar leaves jabbering about the ants and the smoke and the accommodations. By the end of February, they were thicker than I had ever seen them. It was a battle with only two possible outcomes; either he dispersed them, or they would kill him. He declared war on a Monday.

The Old Retired Man's wife had thrown out her daily

allotment of broken bread, and I watched them come in like a band of guerrillas. The point bird landed on the third lowest branch, well out of danger but close enough to get good information about the ground. The second and third came in next, one to the lowest branch, one halfway up the tree. Three more came as soon as those were posted, higher up in the tree, watching the air for predators.

When the last of the clearing crew was in, the point bird shot from the third lowest branch, down across the bread, low enough to make sure what it was but not low enough to be caught by anything. He came out of his flyby on the corner of the porch roof across from the tree. Then the next made his pass, pausing in a clumsy half-hover above the bread, dropping down almost to the ground and then going on by to the other corner of the roof. The third bird down was ground patrol. I never saw one that didn't land reluctantly even though the area had been cleared twice and was probably safe. When she was halfway to the ground, the first half of the flock settled halfway up the closest tree, and a third took backup positions in trees a little further out.

Latecomers lined the roof or took the high points in more distant trees and hoped there would be something left. They came down in twos and threes, and when none of them was set upon, the rest came down at will, walking all over the ground like lizards on two legs, gathering up every edible thing in sight and carrying it off to a perch like frightened thieves.

If anything moved, they rose like a single bird and scattered in small tight groups to trees out beyond the backup contingent, who had already fled. Their approach was always a leap-frogging of contingents; their departure was always a rout. One startled bird could set them all fleeing like one running coward turning an army of cowards into a fleeing mob. But it was a safe, calm day and they stayed there, taking turns walking back and forth over the ground, picking up scraps of leaves, twigs, dirt, anything that might be food and grumbling because it wasn't. The last third of the flock came down afterward and combed the ground for remnants, even though fifty other voracious birds had gone over the same ground for fifteen minutes and departed dissatisfied.

Inevitably those who got in latest took to the roof and drowned their misfortunes in the smoke. The latecomers seemed of two kinds: the optimists who waited their turn on the ground, even though it was obviously going to be fruitless, and the pessimists who knew there was going to be nothing left and tried to get the best positions in line for the chimney. They were always the loudest, even louder than the first birds down, who bragged about their cleverness, or the birds of the closest tree, who complained that the ones on the ground were taking too long. The Blue Jay started his attack with the roofers.

That Monday the flock was the biggest I had seen all winter. The night before had been very cold and there had been snow on the ground only two days before, and the superflock that had formed then was still roosting together. The Blue Jay could not have picked a more dangerous time. The superflock was a hazard to navigation he would ordinarily have left alone.

But I believe February and memories had made him weary of life, and the shame of having failed in his duty weighed him down. The starlings were his last chance to redeem himself with an impossible act or to die honorably. He had only one advantage, and that was his concentration. A hawk diving on starlings will see them scatter, confusing him with too many targets to pursue. But the Blue Jay had an extraordinary focus of attention. He could pick out a single victim and not lose track of him in a crowd. Wherever the rest of the flock went, he would not be distracted from his target. But even armed with rage and despair and hope for salvation, the odds were against him by sheer force of numbers.

I did not realize what he was doing at first, although I had seen him attack starlings before. He came in from above them when the last of the outer-tree skywatch had gone grumbling to their places on the picked-clean ground, and the first of the looters were devouring what they had grabbed. Nobody saw him, and he was in on them before they knew what hit them. He hit the smoke-bathers first. In the flutter to escape, two of them collided and went down the chimney. Only one came back up. The starling he had picked out tried to get airborne, but the Blue Jay hammered him again. The roof line dispersed like a stampede, the groundlings took off into their flocks, and the whole gang went southeast over the houses to the roost tree. The Blue Jay went above them, straight to his highest station at the top of the sky.

From there, he picked out a target in one of the smaller flocks and dove on it. The squad scattered, hoping he would try to follow too many and lose them all, but he was too smart for them and he stayed with the one he had picked and beat it bloody while it tried to flee. Then he went back to the highest tree in the lot and waited.

The starlings settled down to regroup in some maples about three blocks away, but in an hour they were back. He let them settle in again and did it all over. The second sortie drew him two more victims, one on the chimney and another in the clearing crew. This time they went to the roost tree and stayed there. The Blue Jay waited again.

Nobody came back to the yard for more than an hour. They were scared, but they were not panicked yet, and they broke out of the roost tree in small squads again. Little by little, more than half of them went to console themselves in the smoke. It was just what he wanted. For the next two hours, the Blue Jay hit one chimney after another, and everywhere he went, there was hysteria. Every group he hit seemed to think that it was only that one chimney he was protecting, and they took off for the trees until he went away and then came back to a different roof.

The more he attacked them, the more erratic they got, and the more they seemed to need the smoke. He kept at them all day, driving them off their habit one after another until the sun started to go down, and they bunched up in one of the big oaks to the southeast to roost for the night. I don't know where he got the stamina to keep at them the way he did, but when the light started to fail, he let prudence take over. Flying with bad visibility among panicked idiots fleeing in every direction put the odds of a crash too much in their favor. He went back to the lot and waited for morning.

The starlings settled into the roosting tree until the top of it formed a shadowy bloom against the dark gray sky of February dusk. Normally they settled down after a while and then suddenly shut up all at once. But they seemed to go on forever, making a racket that had people coming out of their houses to look. The Blue Jay had broken off his attack, but he was still making his dives in their minds and in their voices until well after sundown. The noise was not only louder but sharper than usual, and the panic in their voices was evident. They all went silent the way they usually do, but not without a few straggling croaks like final complaints after lights out in the barracks. Probably the last thing said was, "Well, he'll be gone in the morning." They were wrong.

The next day when the Old Retired Man's wife threw out her daily bread, the starlings were back. Their contingents came leap-frogging in as always, and there was a thick line on the Old Retired Man's roof. The temperature had gone way down during the night, the way it does out of spite in February, and the starlings were hungry. Most of the flock had gone foraging south, and the hardier ones had gone southeast across the narrower part of the lake to follow the garbage pickups. The lazier or more timid ones stayed in the roost tree or moved in bit by bit toward the Old Retired Man's house and waited for their dole.

The Old Retired Man's wife threw out handfuls of scraps at eight-thirty or nine, when she cleaned up the kitchen. But they were lining up at six, coming and going, taking up spots on the roof and then flying off to other chimneys on roofs nearby that looked more promising. Every house on the block has a fireplace, and every chimney was a doper's paradise for the starlings. The heavier addicts kept themselves together with smoke until the bread came in. The ones who knew they would never be in that first wave that got everything good kept themselves alive dreaming about the ants and summer and folding their wings like capes around the rising stream of smoke. The Blue Jay was already above them waiting.

From time to time, one of them would take a beakful of smoke and touch it under his left wing like an ant, and the others on the roof who saw him would start to shift their feet and edge a little closer to the chimney, bunching up the line in some places and thinning it out in others. It was the Blue Jay's cue to strike.

He knew that the bird who made that habitual gesture was dreamy with the memories of distant sensation, dulled by the habit and the nagging need. He dropped on them like the heavy hand of law and order. His target rarely got its beak out from dragging that invisible ant along the underside of its wing before he struck. He seemed to almost perch on the starling's back and bludgeon its head with that sharp black beak.

If he was a menace on Monday, he was death itself on Tuesday, and his first pass left one fluttering near the base of the chimney and beat another out of the air midway through the yard. He didn't even bother to go back up to his sky station, but went from a dive that drove one starling into the bushes right up so that he struck the next chimney from below. He came up over the lip of the roof out of nowhere and right in between the starlings, who were crouched over the opening of the chimney.

It must have been a starling nightmare to be suddenly dropped out of the warm tingling of fantasy into a reality more terrifying than dream. The roof emptied while the Blue Jay was making his main attack at the chimney, but he always picked one of the squads flying in close order and singled out a second target of opportunity. He was the only jet in a sky full of propellers, and he made bloody mincemeat out of them.

They had numbers, but he had design. He knew where he was going, using the stations of his rounds as bases. The starlings had no idea where he would come from next. It caught them napping every time. He was so quick, Wise Teacher would have watched him with admiration. He came up so swift and silent from a low ground pass on the roof behind mine that he landed between the starlings on the chimney lip before they knew he was there. He glided up, back-pedaled his wings once, and sat down right between two of them. Before they realized he wasn't just another addict, he had struck one, two, three of them and was taking a second jab at the one on his left when the rest broke screeching into the air.

In twenty minutes, he had cleared every roof in the neighborhood. The remnants had gone to the roosting tree, and a bunch had taken all the abuse they were going to and had gone south in search of less haunted territory. The Blue Jay went back to the oak tree and waited for the breakfast crew to come in.

They came a little late and more slowly than usual. A lot of them stopped at the roost tree, which was asquawk whenever anyone landed or took off. The clearing crew took their posts at longer intervals and stayed on their assigned branches longer. The first bird down stayed about half a second and dropped the first piece of bread. It took about twenty minutes instead of ten between the first scout and the main flock. The roof was almost empty. Everyone seemed convinced that the Blue Jay was crazy but only dangerous if someone went on the roofs or near the chimneys, so they stayed in the trees.

The stragglers didn't even bother to come in but stayed in the roost tree and carried on a continual series of groundless warnings to the feeders. The flock took it as sour grapes from the timid and settled to the ground, a little apprehensive but not panicky. But they were on edge, and when I moved the curtain at the window to see them more clearly, the flock rose as one and shot off without hesitation for the roost tree. It took them an hour to get back, and the whole time the Blue Jay was nowhere around.

When they settled the second time, they seemed a little surer of themselves, and the clearing crew worked closer to its usual pace. A few even settled nervously on the garage roof and eyed the chimneys of the houses wistfully. The flock was down and the hoard half-ravished when he struck.

There were about thirty-five birds on the ground and at least twenty in the two trees. It was a more daring and more dangerous maneuver than hitting them on the roofs, because the whole flock raised simultaneously and the chance of accidental collision was enormous. It didn't seem to matter to the Blue Jay; he was committed. He came in like the last of the kamikazes, glad to die for the empire.

He was like a stone thrown in the middle of a pond, and the starlings rippled away from him into the air. But he was a stone that struck the one it was aimed at, and he stayed on his target as she rose into the air and harassed her from all sides while she tried to follow the scattering flock to the roost tree. He did not break off his attack until he was almost in the branches.

They knew he would not pursue them there; it would be too hazardous to make the maneuvers he had to make in a moving attack and still pass between the fingers of the branches. To perch and strike would have made him vulnerable to counterattack as he took off. Every creature feels safer on its own territory, and the starlings, cowards or not, would have been much more likely to fight on their home ground. Going in after them would be virtual suicide.

They were right, and the Blue Jay pulled up and shot past the roost tree, but he was not finished with them. Some of the birds who had not joined the foraging in the yard had taken up compensatory posts on the chimneys near the tree, and the crashes he caused battered at least five too badly to fly before he zoomed back out of their territory. It was an hour before the noise in the roost tree quieted. With the attack on the feeding ground, he had moved from annoyance to nemesis, but there were still those who apparently thought it only a fit of blue-jay temper.

All that bread was still on the ground in the yard if the sparrows had not gotten it, and there were still a good number who were willing to take the risk. Still, it wasn't until late afternoon that the first scouts came in, and it took about five false starts before the clearing crew had secured the area and the main force felt safe enough to come into the trees. There were only about twenty-five birds in all; far more had stayed back in the roost tree. The Blue Jay waited until they were all on the ground before he dropped in among them.

But the secondary group was on the alert and spotted him coming. It was touch and go for a minute. He was in his dive, just about to make his strafing run, when the flock exploded up at him. I thought for certain he would hit one of them and go crashing to the ground, but he did a snap roll a sparrow would have been proud of and slipped between them. The flock took off for home, and the Blue Jay pulled up without a score about halfway there. Then he came back and sat on the edge of the porch roof and dared them to come back. None of them did, and the battle passed into its second night.

It was another cold one, and in the morning, the starlings were hungrier than ever. He had them on the brink of desperation. A bird gets through cold nights by burning up calories, and cutting down on their food threatened them with starvation. A few of the weaker ones had already succumbed, and the flock as a whole was in dangerous shape. The alternatives were not palatable.

The Blue Jay was sitting on their line of supply. They had come to depend on the bread, and they did not have the reserves of energy to forage for what they were losing and still get through a third cold night. The Blue Jay had them with their backs to the wall. It was probably desperation that formed their strategy.

They waited until he left before they moved in. The battle was two days old, and although he had a strategic advantage, the Blue Jay had no reserves. He took a position on the porch roof and dared them to come, and when they didn't, he went down to the ground and ate as much of the bread as he could. The constant attacks were taking their toll of him just as certainly as the starvation was weakening the starlings. He backed off into the lot and allowed them to come in and try to take what was left.

They came in surprisingly fast. The scouts had hardly cleared the area before the whole flock settled into the trees. Half went straight down to the ground, and the other half moved right in to the nearest tree rather than wait in the backup tree as they usually did. I thought they planned to eat quick and get out, but I was wrong. They were waiting for the attack, and the Blue Jay did not disappoint them.

Only the fact that he had circled them and came at them from the direction of the roost tree saved him at all. If he had come straight down at them from above again, they would have gotten him for certain. As it was, he barely escaped. He came in low over the back fence while the scouts and the flock in the trees were watching the sky for him, and he got in a sharp attack on two on the ground before the flock exploded. He went right up after them. It was a mistake.

The half of the flock in the tree closed in on him as he rose and attacked him. They almost smothered him in the air, and only the fact that there were so many of them that they got in each other's way kept them from succeeding. Still, he had a glancing collision with one, and two others made sharp attacks on him before two of them collided and he burst out of the cloud of birds and broke for better position.

He was lucky to get out, but once through the initial cluster, he had the advantage of being faster and more maneuverable. They pursued him, but he was too quick for them, and he was gone before they could bring him down or inflict too much damage on him. Still, he clearly took his lumps, and the momentum had shifted to the starlings. They held the yard; the Blue Jay had been routed if not destroyed, and they were boisterous in their victory.

The Blue Jay was back in the lot awhile later, but he looked winded and worried. The starlings stayed in the yard long after everything was eaten, as if they thought that by occupying the territory continuously, they could make it theirs. They strutted around on the ground, and when the Blue Jay did not come back, about half the flock mobbed the chimneys to try to coax him out. They spread out from their base in the yard in a blitzkrieg, pressing their advantage until they occupied the entire block. They were noisier in victory than they had been in defeat, and their cries seemed full of catcalls and hooting.

For about an hour, it sounded like all the houses in the neighborhood were laughing at him one after another. They held the ground until almost dark, and then they went laughing back to the roosting tree. I felt sorry for the Blue Jay; there were just too many of them. Courage and tenacity can do just so much. When I looked out at him in the fading light, he was sitting in the nesting tree he had not gone near since Carrunner had killed his wife.

I believed then that he was planning his suicide, but I did not think for a minute that he was going to give up, and I was right. The third day the starlings were back bright and early, laughing and joking and shouting to one another, making idle boasts, no doubt, about what they would do to the Jay if he dared show his face. The flock was back in strength, but casualties from the Jay's attacks and from starvation and losses from desertion had reduced their numbers to about fifty.

There were another twenty or so still in the roosting tree who preferred starvation to facing the Blue Jay; no doubt some of them were the walking wounded who had felt his attack firsthand. By ten o'clock, it looked as if the starlings had won. They occupied the yard and the rooftops, and the chimneys were busy as brothels in an occupied city. They had the high ground and numbers; they had the momentum and a workable defense. Even the weather had shifted in their favor. The temperature had gone up into the high fifties, as it will for a day or two just before it plunges to its lowest point. It was all going their way.

The Blue Jay stayed well above them, and the starlings seemed about to organize a death squad to go up after him, but they lacked the guts to do it with less than fifty and it never got out of the talking stage. They would only have gotten in their own way up there anyway, and he would have made them regret it with all that space to maneuver in. Still, he kept them busy, making feints toward them and screaming insults at them as he dove and then pulled up.

At first, he just crossed and recrossed the yard way up above them, like he was on a high reconnaissance patrol. Then he disappeared altogether for a while, but just before the bread was delivered, he was back up there above them again. It sounded to me like they were laughing at him, daring him to come down and get them, but it was really all talk. The Blue Jay knew it, too, and he made some more feints, diving down with a machine-gun burst of *"Jay! Jay! Jay! Jay!"* but pulling up well above the roofs.

The first few times the starlings startled up from the ground, but after a while they only kept a watchful eye on him. Obviously he was afraid to attack, but they knew he was crazy and there was always the chance he might make a real effort. I was glad he was showing some sense, but I was a little disappointed in him. I didn't want to see him get hurt, but I hated to hear the racket the starlings were making at his expense. The racket was probably their undoing, although I would like to think that when the Blue Jay disappeared, he went for reinforcements. Still, it's more likely the starlings brought destruction on themselves.

They settled on the bread and made a festival of devouring it. Even so, every bird in the trees and half of those on the ground kept looking up at the Blue Jay's dives, half-apprehensively, half-scornfully. If they looked on the ground at all, it was only to pick up the nearest piece of bread. They walked from piece to piece, laughing and joking. Nobody looked at the bushes next to the house; nobody had any idea what was there except the Blue Jay, and he was doing his best to keep their minds off the ground with his futile acrobatics. The Orange Cat caught them flat-footed.

She had hands Wise Teacher would have approved of, and she could turn quicker than Carrunner. She caught two on the ground and a third by going up on her hind legs to swat it out of the air. Her shriek was sharper than her claws, and it sliced the air in pieces as far away as the roosting tree. If the Blue Jay had been a terror, the Orange Cat was terror itself.

The starlings almost bumped into each other a dozen times trying to get airborne in their rush to get out of harm's way. They didn't even leap up, they just took off in a rising line for the roost tree, and those whose first move had carried them in the opposite direction had turned in the direction of home before they cleared the rooftops. They flew for the tree as if the cat were flying right behind them. They were less a flock than a mob trying to get out the only exit in a fire-filled room.

A third of the flock passed the tree altogether and kept on going. Maniac blue jays were one thing, cats were another. They had had enough of adventure and were going *any*place else. The parts of the flock that stopped at the roost tree jammed into the topmost branches. They were crazy with fear, and the tree was pandemonium. Birds squeezed out of the crown of the tree, swore, and landed on lower branches only momentarily before trying to force their way back into the crown. They had been a flock when they ambushed the Blue Jay, but they were a bickering, divided pack of cowards at heart, and the Orange Cat had reminded them that they were starlings after all and not eagles.

The last of them came fluttering in, trying to find a place to land and pursued by none other than the Blue Jay himself, pecking and jabbing at them on the dead run. Diving out of his way, they crashed onto branches, bumping others off and causing more panic. The tree exploded as some of them realized that the Blue Jay was back. Their cries reached out as if to pull their roostmates to safety, then froze in the air as the Blue Jay came right in after them. He might as well have been the Orange Cat.

The entire flock burst out of the tree in all directions;

some went spinning halfway to the ground, bouncing off each other to avoid certain crashes with the branches. A hawk could have landed among them with less effect. Airborne, the flock disintegrated into a hundred pieces, each streaking toward any destination as long as it was far away. The Blue Jay chased the nearest with a stream of invective for a block or so, but in a twinkling, the flock was gone, shattered.

The Blue Jay came back and sat in the roost tree at the very top of the highest branch and waited for them to come back. A few of the hardier ones made a flyover about two hours later, but the Blue Jay hopped from one branch to another and they veered off back toward safer roosts across the lake without even slowing down. The next morning he was still in that tree, waiting for them to come back.

The Old Retired Man's wife came out and scattered her bread for the needy. The sparrows came and ate most of it. There were no starlings on the block. The rooftops were clear. The chimneys trailed wisps of smoke into the air but no birds leaned over the ticklish rise. It was another fine warming day. About eleven, the Blue Jay came down and ate what was left of the bread. It was a big meal, a flock of starlings' worth, but he had a fine appetite.

When he was finished, he flew up onto my roof and went poking in the rain gutter. He thrashed in the dead leaves like somebody rooting in a closet for an important keepsake he has been hoarding for a long time, waiting for a special occasion. He stopped thrashing and looked one way, then the other. Then he hopped a foot to his left and checked the coordinates again. The leaves flew again, and when he raised his head, he had an acorn in his beak. Then he spread his wings like a vision and swooped to the ground he had won for all blue jays.

Right in the middle of the yard, he set the acorn down and cocked his head, right, then left, then right, marking its location forever in his files as if he planned to come back someday and sit in the branches of the tree he was certain would grow there. Then he cocked his head again and jabbed the spade of his beak under the thawing grass. He had to strike it hard a dozen times. It was tough work, and some instinct must have told him that it was the wrong time of the year to be doing it, but I believe he was performing a sacred act because it was all he had to commemorate a historic event.

He went at it with a vengeance until he had kicked up a pocket under the grass. Then he picked up the acorn and poked it into the hole, took it out again and fitted it back in, prodding and poking until it fit perfectly. Then he tapped the grass down over it, closing the turf over the tree that landlords of the property yet unborn would sit in.

He looked right and left again and hopped back a few feet as if he was looking up at the tree that would one day stand there. Then he made one last climb straight to the roof of the property, made a small circle and flew north, where the winters were harder and there was property tougher and more in need of a strong jay to set it right. He flew hard and straight, with a lift every so often that looked like joy, and he did not look back.

Water Walker

For days after Carrunner went out on the ice to die, Wise Teacher went listlessly about his rounds. Sometimes there were things which escaped his attention, but very little escaped his notice. He would start to investigate something in the lot and halfway through it, he would wander away from it aimlessly. When he did, he always ended up at the lake. Maybe he wondered whether he too would succumb to that irreversible stillness into which Carrunner had disappeared. Maybe he looked down across the ice wondering if Carrunner would come back. I doubt it, though; he had investigated too many deaths in his tour of duty not to know that nothing comes back, at least not as it was.

His lethargy seemed the culmination of a process that had been going on since Carrunner had come back from the vet's, broken in mind and body. The division between

them had not been irrevocable. It was well within the code
for a headstrong apprentice to strike out on his own too
soon. Properly handled, it could have been a lesson, if the
Blue Jay's vengeance had not shattered all reasonable
expectations. If Wise Teacher had taken Carrunner's
defection seriously, he would not have altered the times of
his rounds so that they would not compete, and when
Carrunner provoked him, he would have driven him out of
the neighborhood. Instead, Wise Teacher had given Carrunner the opportunity to make it on his own. If he had
failed, there would have been only a small charge for
readmission.

In the meantime, Wise Teacher had not taken on
another apprentice—although it must be admitted that
there were no suitable candidates. There were several
young and aggressive cats, but none was a Seal Point, and
none was even Siamese. No doubt his bearing and even his
presence in the neighborhood taught all cats something,
but the secrets of his teachings were not for ordinary cats.
They did not have the concentration for it.

It was true that Carrunner had been easily distracted,
but he had had a capacity for learning the others lacked.
He could be guided. Among the mixed breeds and the
American shorthairs within walking distance of Wise
Teacher's domain, there was none he would consider. If he
had wished, he might have taken on several and organized
them into an efficient force, but there was that inevitable
aloofness that was part of being something special that
kept him from fraternizing well. The species had other
plans for him.

Seal-Point reserve kept him always just a little beyond
the reach of all but his own kind. It was necessary to his
training of young Siamese. What he had to pass along was
very special, and it could not be given to just anyone. A
certain kind of mind was necessary to grasp his lessons, a
special kind of intelligence. Carrunner was born with a

head start on both. He had a common genetic background with Wise Teacher; they did not think exactly alike, but there were similarities in the quality of their thoughts, in their styles of organizing information that made communication with anyone else seem like translation. Simply being Siamese had given Carrunner a commonality of mind with Wise Teacher that none of the other candidates could match.

Wise Teacher must have missed that. Nevertheless, with Carrunner finally gone, he would have to make a choice. He could take no apprentice at all and leave his old age to chance, but that was not consistent with his style. He could have taken on a series of apprentices, using them to cut his work load and lengthen the time he could live before he burned himself out. He could go through a series of mediocre apprentices, teaching them as much as they had the capacity to learn, using them as he had Carrunner as the price of tuition.

Or he could find a suitable successor to Carrunner, a special cat he could pass everything on to. There are two drives that move the individual to do the species's work, and they both tend toward immortality. The first is by progeny. If Purrfect Moving Mind had been allowed to free Wise Teacher's litter into the neighborhood, he would have had no problem. He would have trained each as far as their capacity would allow and would have selected the most outstanding to teach the choicest of his secrets. In that way, when he himself had followed Carrunner into the stillness, some portion of his traits would continue and would create successors who would themselves pass on the attributes that the species found important.

The information in his genes had its own impetus to be passed on, but there is another kind of immortality which the species requires, and that is the immortality of knowledge, not in its genetic form but in the form of culture, in the form of the personal transmission of important survival skills. Wise Teacher was driven to have apprentices just as surely as he was driven up that precarious branch to Purrfect Moving Mind.

Habits of character—the prudence, the meticulousness, the ability to focus on a single event without losing sight of the whole in which it played only a part—were techniques that could only be passed on by teaching. Just as he could leave a genetic endowment which would further the species, so he could leave a set of understandings he himself had taught. What he had been in the process of passing on to Carrunner would be lost if he did not find someone to pass it on to.

The kind of specialized knowledge he had inevitably went hand in hand with a drive to express it, a compulsion to pass that kind of information on. In the packet of traits he had inherited, there was one which made him pass on what he had learned. Survival of the species required it. Anyone who is a strong enough bet to advance the breed would have to have the compulsion to tell someone else of their kind what they had learned. Birds sing for no greater reason, and it is the way they express what it is like to be part of the species that attracts mates, protects territories, builds nests, and keeps the flock together. The quality of mind that allowed Wise Teacher to accomplish as much as he did went inevitably with a need to pass on his wisdom, to train successors to pass on what might be lost in the transmission of the genes.

Probably seeing it assimilated was its own reward. Whether the messages carried by his genes took effect or not was something he might never know; the feedback of teaching was far more immediate. When Wise Teacher taught Carrunner a lesson, he could see right away the effect of his efforts. There was a certainty to the successful transmission of knowledge that made it worthwhile.

There were economic advantages, as well. Two could eventually hunt both things and information with the efficiency of three. A lot more could be learned with an apprentice. Not only could the routine be passed on to him without sacrificing any information, but the divergence of approach would make Wise Teacher see his own actions from a new perspective. In order to maneuver Carrunner toward better understanding, Wise Teacher had to be able to think like him, and in doing so, he learned new ways of thinking which would not otherwise have occurred to him.

Carrunner had weaknesses to be sure, but when Wise Teacher looked at the world through them, they became strengths because they gave him new insights into the overall pattern. Learning how to keep a dozen steps ahead of Carrunner gave him two kinds of mind, his own and Carrunner's. Before he did anything, he had to think how Carrunner would approach it and how he would react to each situation.

Part of the exchange of ideas came from the reverse, that Carrunner was forced to try to think like Wise Teacher in order to keep up with him. He was forced to understand what was going on the way Wise Teacher understood it. The fact that that way was so different from his own made him a creature of two minds like Wise Teacher, less only in degree. The advantages he gained from two-mindedness would lead him eventually to take on his own apprentice, to pass on what he knew.

Having an apprentice kept Wise Teacher from becoming stereotyped in his thinking. Having learned prudence and analysis on his own, he learned impulsiveness and intuition from his apprentice. The association was made for survival. It kept Wise Teacher from becoming stagnant, in return for passing on insights that improved the likelihood of survival for the species.

Culture transmits a second message, and the teaching of culture—what it is like to be a particular species, whether it is Seal Point, blue jay or human—is a primary activity of every species. The old teach the young how to be effective cats, or dogs, or humans. In doing so, they not only pass on traits that make survival for all more likely, but they pass on a specific way of seeing the world that is unique to themselves.

Every teacher has his idiom; everyone who passes on culture filters it through his own experience and his own way of approaching things. All animals pass on culture, the noninheritable points of survival that are peculiar to the species. Culture is the part of being a cat that does not get transmitted in the genes, that has to be taught and learned. At any point, the process can fail only if a whole generation perishes; only if all cats cease to exist will the process of what is handed down from one to the other be lost.

The two strains go together. As long as there are cats, they will teach their offspring their understanding of what is necessary for them to be a cat. In species where the young are not directly reared, there is a double function. Those who have the capacity teach others as they would their own offspring. Teaching culture, like passing on genetic traits, is inherently pleasurable. It feels good to make more cats, and it feels good to teach cats how to live like cats more elegantly.

But there is a built-in selectivity in that regard, as well. Wise Teacher was more likely to teach someone like himself than someone who could not easily follow the way his mind worked. At the very least, he would tend to be found in the company of someone like himself, and Carrunner was not entirely different from Wise Teacher when Wise Teacher was young. The other cats were very unlike him.

Still, Wise Teacher had the same urge to take on an apprentice that the Orange Cat had to make kittens. It might not have been as strong an urge, but it was unmistakably there. When he sat looking out at the lake, he must have been thinking about how the process had inexplicably gone awry. All the time he had invested in

Carrunner, not merely to train him into a perfect hunting partner, but in passing on knowledge which would die with him otherwise, had come to nothing.

Part of the function of the loneliness that drew him to the lake was the impetus to pass on what he knew, to share it with another like himself so that it could be passed on to even later Seal Points. The need to have an apprentice was irresistible, but the fact that he would have to leave so much untaught with any of the new apprentices must have made him despair of beginning again. He was getting older, and there must have been some question in his mind about whether all he had accumulated of value could even *be* passed on. It took a minimum time to teach what it had taken him a maximum time to learn, but there was no lessening that minimum. Even if he could find a pupil as promising as Carrunner, there was no guarantee that he could bring him along to the end of his training.

There was no doubt that he could take any of the young cats and teach it to hunt better, to live independently among the pitfalls and dangers of man and dog. But the process of exposing a novice to each situation in a particular way so that the search for the pattern-in-all-things could emerge as a way of thinking, a way of being, took a long time. Completed, the task would leave a second cat as aware of the world and its ramifications as Wise Teacher. But there was experience after experience that could not be explained and had to be lived and often relived to be understood.

Wise Teacher had no books to rely on; he had to create each situation or take advantage of any naturally occurring one and make it into a lesson. And yet a decision would have to be made, and soon, because the impulse to teach what he knew was growing stronger the longer he went without doing it, and his own way of looking at the world was narrowing day by day. He needed the sense of wonder only an apprentice could bring to things to keep him from glossing over the basic and important things long usage had made stale. The dilemma brought him always to the lake, as if Carrunner would rise from the ice and resolve it. He sat for hours looking out across the ice, trying to figure out what to do next. He was fortunate that the Orange Cat gave him an omen.'

When the Orange Cat turned the tide of battle against the starlings, she did a peculiar thing, something I had read about but had doubted. She took the three birds she had killed and carried them one at a time through the fence and across the back of my yard to a place beside my house where Wise Teacher always came on his daily patrol. He had a path alongside my house that took him under the branches of some shrubs, beside a huge rhubarb plant, and out under the place where the living room overhangs the foundation.

He always went that same route, pausing just at the edge of the shadow of the overhang and looking up the rest of the driveway. Then he would pass along close to the wall and between the trash cans, or where the trash cans would be if the trash men put them back properly. If they were in place, he would look out between them at the backyard before he crossed it and then go off down a narrow corridor between the fence and the garage of the house to the left of the Catkeepers.

About halfway across my backyard, he always gave one quick look at the window where Purrfect Moving Mind used to sit. She was never there after the Catkeepers realized she was pregnant. What they did with her, I don't really know, but I know that she had the kittens because I saw her holding them one at a time by the scruff of the neck at the attic window, as if showing them how far down it was and what a brave climb their father had made.

The Catkeepers put an ad in the paper for Siamese kittens awhile later but it said nothing about pedigree, so I am sure they knew Wise Teacher was the father. They put an ad in the real estate section about the same time, and they seem to have moved out, although the house has not been bought by anybody else. Either Mr. Catkeeper got a new job or they moved to another town to cover up Purrfect Moving Mind's disgrace.

Probably they have married her off a couple of litters' worth to the cats of foreign dignitaries and are showing the best of her litters in cat shows in some other city. Wise Teacher did not stop and he did no more than glance up at that window, but he glanced every time, and I believe he thought about her when he looked although he never let it distract him from what he was doing.

He had no interest in other cats. There was a female Siamese down toward the lake, but she was a Blue Point, and I believe he had more important things on his mind. He looked up at the tree he had climbed every time, too, but it was a look of puzzlement, as if he wondered whatever had possessed him to do such a foolhardy thing. Summer was probably decades ago in his reckoning, and the tragedies that had flown past since then must have made it seem like centuries to him. Still, he paused and glanced and went on about his business every day.

The path was always the same. I could walk it myself in his footprints if it were not so hard on the knees. Every cat that came up my driveway avoided that path, even though it was the most secure route. I suppose he had marked it with unmistakable chemical signatures that not only declared it to be a main route of Wise Teacher but one he would guard against intrusion, by force if necessary. I imagine any cat foolhardy enough to challenge him on his home turf would only have had to walk along that path and sign their own name over his to provoke a fight. But none of them ever did. A cat's nose is not a dog's, but it is a good deal better than a human being's, and although the path is invisible, every cat knew it was there.

I know the Orange Cat knew it, because she laid all

three birds in a row so exactly and unmistakably in the middle of it that it could not be coincidence. It is unusual for a cat to kill so many birds at once, but to line them up, laying them all with their heads pointing south and their tails pointing north so that they crossed the path at a perfect right angle, goes beyond unusual. She undoubtedly left them for Wise Teacher, although even he did not know why when he found them.

He knew immediately who left them. If his nose had not told him, he could have guessed after turning them over one by one with his paw and examining the wounds. Every cat strikes in its own unique way, just the way every boxer throws the same right cross differently in a different combination of punches. Wise Teacher could tell who made the claw marks on a tree by their angle and their sequence.

When he turned the birds over, he looked as if he thought excellent craftsmanship had been involved in their killing. I have no doubt he was impressed. Three birds, all killed at the same time between one of his rounds and the next, was quite a feat. To get one bird takes more than an amateur. Even Wise Teacher is not always successful, and Carrunner made a kill one time in a dozen. Three at a time was nothing short of remarkable. Almost as remarkable as the fact that someone had put them in his path. Even I could tell it was an offer of some kind.

The Orange Cat would certainly not have left them as a challenge. If she were a male, the act could have been construed as a threat, but the meaning of a gesture, like everything else, Wise Teacher knew, came out of its context, the relationship between the events surrounding it and the identities involved. A strange tom might have left them as a message that said, "Get out of town by sundown." Signed: " The Fastest Cat in the West." But coming from the Orange Cat, they had to mean something different.

Wise Teacher poked at the birds, walked away, and then

came back and poked at them some more. They seemed to puzzle him more than anything else in weeks. It was unlikely that she left them as a calculated insult, a way of telling him he was slipping. The circumstances that would give even someone as quick as Wise Teacher the chance to do such a thing were few and far between.

They were all starlings, so he was sure it must have something to do with whatever had been going on between the Blue Jay and the starlings. But he did not know exactly what that was. It made the dead birds bother him even more. He did not pass them once in the next day and a half without poking around them, trying to figure it out. Probably realizing how little he knew about their origin made him realize how badly his intelligence gathering had fallen off. There was a time when he would not only have known what was going on but would have been able to capitalize on it as the Orange Cat apparently had.

I believe that what he admired was less the handiwork on the birds, which was clearly inferior to his own though quite good, than the strategy that must have been involved and the data about the neighborhood that must have been behind it. Each time he poked at the birds, he must have realized how his attention had been slipping, how much time he had been wasting at the lake.

He spent hours at the lake in the weeks after Carrunner went out onto the ice. It was probably the place where he went to confront his mortality. He rarely went down the steep bank to the water. Carrunner used to go down the bank all the time, running pell-mell so that his momentum would actually take him into the water and wet his feet. The thought was abhorrent to Wise Teacher. He would shiver involuntarily whenever it happened, and he shivered the same way when Carrunner was no longer there to make his reckless descent. I believe the memory of it made him shiver.

The rest of the time, he sat like a china cat at the top of

the bank, looking to his left where the lake gets shallow. A big iron pipe runs under the road from the higher lake on the other side. Carrunner used to bring him rats from the pipe, but Wise Teacher went there rarely. He had an aversion to water that seemed to be based on fear. Probably there was a kitten's terror behind it all, some plunge under the water into that silent, smothering brightness from which only a mother's watchful eye could see him or reach in to scoop him out. The lake was a mystery to Wise Teacher, soft and deadly at certain times, rigidly hard at others.

He had seen Carrunner walk on the ice and suddenly drop into the water when a small piece of it broke off. He had howled relentlessly until Carrunner had managed to pull himself back up onto the ice. The thought of it made him shiver involuntarily, as if he were cold and wet. He would no more walk out on the ice than he would intentionally swim, and yet the lake fascinated him. Of all the things that changed in his domain, the lake changes most, offers the most surprises, provides the greatest dangers. Dogs are drawn to it. People come and go from its bank; total strangers come and leave the remnants of fish and disappear without a trace, never to return.

It was always the one part of his domain where Carrunner had the advantage. It was one reason he had taken the apprentice to begin with. Before Carrunner, he had had to force himself down the bank to prowl at the edge of the water. There was always too much information below the level of the road to ignore the place entirely, but it was always a place that made him uncomfortable, a place he was afraid of.

The water was a mystery, too, hard as the street in winter, and yet in summer, it gave way before a striking hand like the dark mystery of his shadow. With Carrunner, he needed to go down the bank only once every few days. Carrunner could be sent to tell whether anything had been importantly disturbed. Half of the time, Carrunner would report no change, and he would be spared the necessity of forcing himself down the bank.

He went down it only once or twice a week after Carrunner picked it as his leaving place. I am sure the impulse to take another apprentice entered his mind every time he went down. The necessity to overcome that fear must have nagged at him every time as well, but he was not desperate enough to do so. Still, he always went there when something was bothering him.

The three birds sent him there to think, and he sat on the top of the bank in full view of the street, looking down and across the lake. On the far bank, which is just as steep, there are more houses with backyards full of trees, but for all he cares, they might as well be on the moon. He has investigated part of the far side of the lake, crossing by way of the road and coming down the far bank, but he has no claims there, and it is of only peripheral interest to him. It is the lake itself that fascinates him—the water, which he abhors, the danger, and the association with Carrunner.

The bank is a world of information, a resource of food, and a place full of adventures. Carrunner loved it. Wise Teacher went to it more out of compulsion. When he sat there motionless, the birds must have been on his mind, because his tail kept twitching back and forth, back and forth, as if it was pacing behind him, trying to figure it out. The possibilities were hard to arrange. Communication by symbol is not always precise even among users of words, and among cats, it is a little used but enormously important form of speech.

Everything about the incident was peculiar. If the birds had been simply arranged in a neat row where they had been killed, it might have been only an expression of sheer elation, a desire to show the world what a great thing had been done. Sheer exuberance could have caused it. But it was not a likely explanation for their arrangement on the path.

A cat with young should have taken the food back to them. Undoubtedly she had already taught them to hunt, but although they were almost ready to go out on their own, they could not have been bringing in so much food that the birds would not have been missed. Leaving them there was clearly a sacrifice. Hunting for five hungry mouths for so long, even if they were almost self-support-ing, would have made Wise Teacher lean, and there was no doubt the Orange Cat herself could have used the protein.

Certainly a remarkable event like that required some gesture, but she could have eaten parts of the birds and still have had enough left to make her statement. Besides, the birds had been left directly across his path. The message had clearly been meant for him. The discrepancies gnawed at him.

There was a possible explanation, but it was farfetched. Carrunner had done a similar thing when he had applied as apprentice. He had left a field mouse on the path at a particular time, then had appeared there at that same time every day when Wise Teacher came by. He would wait patiently for Wise Teacher to go by, and then he would cross the path and go on his own way. He kept up that routine until Wise Teacher finally stopped and looked him over. When he laid a second mouse across the path, Wise Teacher picked it up and carried it off. It seemed to be a signal for Carrunner to follow, and from then on, they were master and apprentice.

But it made no sense for the Orange Cat to be making that kind of gesture. Surely all the times he had driven her from her spying on him should have told her that any professional association between them was out of the question. It crossed his mind that she was unmistakably the most intelligent of the neighborhood cats, and three birds showed clearly that she would be no drain when it came to hunting. And it was also true that she had served a partial apprenticeship at a distance, watching everything she could of what he had tried to teach Carrunner. It was not impossible that the thought of becoming his apprentice had crossed her mind, but it was unthinkable to Wise Teacher, and she should have known it. There was far too much against it.

First, she was too old. Carrunner had been further into youth than Wise Teacher would have liked, but he would have been in his prime a long time after Wise Teacher began to slow down, and the hunting association between them would have paid dividends well into old age. The Orange Cat was almost as mature as Wise Teacher; they would get old together, fade almost simultaneously. There was no possible return for his investment of time and effort.

No doubt she was a fine hunter and a good intelligence gatherer. She could not have been in the proper place to kill three birds if she did not have an intimate knowledge of what was going on in the neighborhood. But he had no need of those skills at the moment, and when age had made him dependent, she would be as useless as he was.

Age alone would have disqualified her, but there were other considerations, not the least of which was sex. There would be days when she was of no use at all, bent and twisted by her heat, and even if she could overcome those tense drives before which she was helpless, she would still attract every male with a nose to his territory. The competitors in Wise Teacher's niche set their schedules around his, made sure they did not cross a path until he had disappeared safely around a corner. He knew they were there, but they stayed out of his sight and avoided confrontations except at the nightly meeting place, where it was by custom agreed to meet without hostility.

The Orange Cat would draw them like flies on a melting

ice cream cone, and even though he had no interest in her sexually, he would have to defend his territory against a dozen males as preoccupied with her needs as Carrunner would have been. The thought of undisciplined toms wandering freely around his territory, of dozens of mixed breeds drawn to her scent and made a little crazy by it, was outrageous.

Worse, she would be almost useless for weeks before she littered and for months afterward, not to mention that she would add the burden of all those hungry mouths until they were weaned and ready to go on their own. That kind of drain on his energies when he began to slow down with age would be suicidal. Probably she would be past littering by then, but the batches of kittens that would suck away his energies in the meantime would hurry him into a premature old age. The more he thought of it, the more of an insult it must have seemed, and the more his tail went back and forth, back and forth.

If she was as intelligent as she must suppose to think herself capable of understanding the rigors of his teaching, then she should certainly have understood that it was unthinkable, that she had nothing to offer in the long run and only problems in the short term. Carrunner, for all his faults, had brought distinct advantages with him and potentials that were even more important. The Orange Cat was a disaster. It was an insult that she should even make such overtures to him.

I believe he was disappointed that she did not have the good sense and breeding to understand that herself and had decided to give her a severe chastisement when he saw her again. He began to clean himself into a calm, licking his paws and his forearms, smoothing and cleaning his coat along his back. By the time he had finished, he was less angry.

No doubt it was something he should have expected from a mixed breed, a peasant. Quite probably she had some purebred in her ancestry somewhere or she would not have had the intelligence she had, but she was clearly deficient in understanding if she did not realize automatically that there could be no meeting of the minds between a Seal Point and a mixed breed.

Even if she were a male, even if she were young and strong, clever if not wise, even if she was the best of a bad lot of applicants, she could not hope to understand the subtleties of his teaching if she did not understand that there was a line between them that was uncrossable, a demarcation of breed that was more important than any similarities. If she had had even the smallest drop of Seal Point in her, she would have realized that from the start. If she had even a drop of Siamese, she would have realized that she would always be a waste of his time.

The thought must have annoyed him all over again because he began cleaning his coat again. Every time an angry thought passed through his head, his tail would start to bush out. First it lashed back and forth as the agitation increased, and then when he got angry, it would fluff out, not into the brush of imminent attack, but thick enough to be noticeable to anyone who looked. It happened every time he saw the birds and every time he went to the bank directly afterward.

If only they had been left by some young, strong Seal Point, or if only Carrunner had left them and would pop out of the bushes halfway up the bank in his old form, with his knowing swagger and a cry that said that the whole thing had been a trick to teach Wise Teacher a lesson. But that was impossible. He looked out across the lake to where he had come every day to watch Carrunner's dark, stiff form on the ice until it had disappeared.

The ice had melted twice since then and had begun to melt again two days before. It had disappeared under a sheet of water that rippled slowly across from the far shore. But Wise Teacher did not have Carrunner's intimate knowledge of ice, and as far as he was concerned, it was gone. When he looked out across the lake, his tail stopped moving and he hunched forward to see better. The Orange Cat was walking toward him across the water.

The water stopped just above her claws. He watched her stride steadily forward as if she was walking on land. What he saw beside her explained everything. For an instant, he thought it was Carrunner come back, but it was only a young male cat.

Covering its face where Wise Teacher's face was dark were the stripes of the Orange Cat, and on his front and rear legs where the boots of a Seal Point Siamese should be were the strange, muted orange stripes again. But the rest of him was clearly Siamese—the shape of the head, the lean body, the flexible, expressive tail. The Orange Cat trotted across the water, making little splashings with her feet. The young cat trotted behind her most of the way, but it had a swagger Wise Teacher could not mistake. When it trotted ahead of the Orange Cat, it never got more than a few body lengths before it slowed down, just as Carrunner would have.

When they were two thirds of the way across, the Orange Cat stopped. The youngster stopped as well. She came over to him and nudged him forward. He took a few steps and stopped. She looked up the bank at Wise Teacher, and he understood the gift of the birds that had plagued him. He did not need to hear her call to know that she was offering the boy as an apprentice, that she left the birds as a statement of his pedigree on his maternal side.

The parts of him that were not Siamese were nevertheless not ordinary. He was obviously an apprentice who would not only be able to understand the peculiar quirkiness of Siamese thought but to take advantage of it in a unique way, one that could carry Wise Teacher into a bountiful old age and an easeful death.

But the Orange Cat was not above a twist of arrogance

herself, and she did not bring the youngster all the way to
Wise Teacher. She left him sitting a good thirty body
lengths out on the water and gave a cry that was not
supplication but a challenge. Then she turned and left
without looking back. The challenge was clear. She was
telling Wise Teacher that if he wanted the boy, he would
have to prove himself worthy by coming out onto the ice to
get him.

She could have left the young cat with the birds; instead,
she left him with something more important, a mystery.
Wise Teacher watched her trot back across the water
toward the far bank. At the far side, she crouched for a
moment and then made an enormous leap to the shore. In
an instant, she had disappeared into the underbrush of the
far shore and was gone. The young cat did not move the
whole time, did not even turn his head to look over his
shoulder at his departing mother. Such partings were
inevitable.

Wise Teacher admired his courage, but he admired the
young cat's discipline more. It sat on the cold water as if it
were on dry ground, and it did not move. The Orange Cat
had already begun its training, and it had more capacity
than Wise Teacher could have hoped for. He doubted that
Carrunner would have been able to sit that motionless in
that much discomfort; he was not even sure he himself
would have been able to do it at that age. He was so taken
by its concentration that he almost ignored the fact that it
was sitting on water.

The Orange Cat had made it clear that he would not
move until Wise Teacher came for him, and Wise Teacher
knew that if he was not able to conquer his fear and try to
walk on the water, he was not a strong enough master for
the young cat to follow. He went slowly down the bank.
The water looked ominous. He thought of its depth, its
smothering brightness as it closed over the head, and the
fur rose along his back.

When he got to the edge, he put his right hand into the water and gingerly put his weight on it. It went in halfway up his arm. He jerked it back with a shock. The water was water, and yet the young cat sat on it as easily as if it were land. The mystery made him take a step back, shaking his wet arm. The fur was cold and it stuck up in matted clumps. He smoothed it with his tongue and looked out at the young cat. He was a prize indeed, an apprentice who knew something his teacher did not; a remarkable thing, truly wondrous. A pupil like that was worth a great risk.

A cat who could walk on water was an amazing thing, and yet he knew that there had to be an explanation for it. If only he could get enough information, he would be able to figure it out. He walked along the edge of the water, where the softening mud shimmered with ice crystals. He poked at the piles of shivered ice along the edge of the bank and looked out at the young cat. The cat sat motionless, waiting for him. There was no need to introduce him; his name was clearly Water Walker, and he could go where Wise Teacher himself could not.

Wise Teacher paced back to his right and leaned his head out over the water until his whiskers touched the surface. The Orange Cat had left him a lesson he understood in all its complexity. She had left him a miracle apprentice who came with a supply of knowledge as tuition, and at the same time pointed out to Wise Teacher the insufficiency of his own knowledge. His fear of the water had limited his domain to one side of the lake, had kept him stunted in his scope.

There were things even the lowliest mixed breed knew about the world that he could not know because he limited his intelligence gathering to the edges of the lake and an occasional foray around the road end. Events that shaped on its far side were unknown to him until they broke on the shore of his territory. The Orange Cat could walk on water because she had information he did not, because her range was wider, because she was not limited by a kitten's experience, a childhood fear. She knew a world beyond Wise Teacher's, and she had left him a key to it in return for the knowledge he alone could give to Carrunner's son. But she had left him only one way to get it.

The ice he could not see stopped just outside the reach of his paw, but there was no way to be certain of it. He looked across the lake to where the Orange Cat had left the ice with that peculiarly long leap. He fitted it into a pattern, put it together with what little he knew of ice, and came to the only conclusion available to him. The ice must be under the water, and the shards of ice crystal that mounded in front of him were the parts of it that had broken off.

He examined everything he knew about the lake in winter, and he came up with the memory he needed. Once Carrunner had gone down to the edge of the lake while it was solidly white with ice and had drunk from a crack between the ice and the shore. He remembered watching the ice shrink back from the land day by day before it began to break up into pieces. He had seen rain cover it and dissolve it, and he had seen it turn gradually soft so that even Carrunner would not chance crossing it. Sometimes, if there was a long enough cold spell and then a sudden period of warmth, the ice melted on top only. It made him certain that the ice must be only an inch or so under the water. But there was still no way to tell how far out it began.

He crouched on the bank. Water Walker cocked his head toward him as if he could not understand what was keeping him. Wise Teacher could see Carrunner's impatience held tightly under control in Water Walker. Intelligence told him it was safe to jump, fear told him it was the smothering end he had always dreaded. The leap he made was a leap of faith.

It was a remarkably long leap, and the water shocked his

feet up above the rounded turrets of his claws as he landed. He felt them strike the ice a little higher than he had expected, and it made his landing look a little clumsy, but he recovered quickly. He took a moment to reestablish his dignity, and walked toward Water Walker. The young cat watched him come with an air of expectation, as if waiting for a command.

But he did not move. He stayed where he had been told, did what he had obviously been taught. It was a feat that left Wise Teacher impressed. He walked around Water Walker, looking him over as if he might still reject him after all and leave him to make his own way in the world. There was a certain distance that had to be kept between student and teacher, a necessary respect that could not be broached.

He leaned close and inspected the curious markings. If they had been black, there was no doubt that Water Walker would have been as close to Wise Teacher's kind as Carrunner had been. There was not an overwhelming importance to the markings; certainly a Seal Point was better, but there was a good deal to be said for Blues, and there was obviously much to be gotten from the new breed as well, because the youngster did not succumb to the temptation to look back over his shoulder to see what Wise Teacher was doing.

Wise Teacher looked at the curve of his head, the fine, lean strength of his back. He liked the way the cat held his tail up out of the water without seeming to make an effort of it. There was an elegance to it that was clearly aristocratic and innate. The youngster was obviously the best prospect around, and he would need a new apprentice with a whole new world to explore. He walked back toward the bank a few steps; Water Walker stayed where he had been told. Wise Teacher looked back over his shoulder and walked a little further.

The young cat stretched a foot forward tentatively. Wise

Teacher looked back again and made a sound that was halfway between exasperation and command. He seemed to be saying, "Well, come along, what are you waiting for?" Water Walker trotted after him, keeping a couple of body lengths behind. When he was at the outer range of his leaping ability from the bank, Wise Teacher crouched. He had no idea where the edge of the ice was. Water Walker walked up beside him. Wise Teacher looked over at him and nonchalantly stretched a foot forward, feeling for the edge of the ice. Then he brought his body up to his foot. He looked along the bank to be sure nothing was waiting for him to land. Then he stretched both feet out in front of him and bent his back as if limbering up for a jump, but I believe he was really feeling his way closer to the edge so that he could be sure the youngster could make it.

It was a longish jump, but it would be a good first test, and it would tell him a great deal about his apprentice no matter how it turned out. He crouched again and leapt for the bank. The ice crystals crunched under his feet as he came down. His fur was wet and he did not like it. The price of new knowledge was apparently steep, but he was willing to pay it.

He looked back at the youngster, who crouched uncertainly on the water. The look was easily understood. If he was going to follow Wise Teacher, he would have to keep up the pace, and he would have to trust Wise Teacher's judgment. Water Walker tightened his crouch and sprang for the shore.

But the jump was too far and he fell short. Wise Teacher leaned back out over the water and grabbed him by the scruff of the neck like a kitten and pulled him out. He set him on the cold, ice-caked mud with a sound that seemed like a human sigh. There was a long way to go. He had no idea just how long until Water Walker shook himself with a frenzy, splashing water all over Wise Teacher. Wise Teacher roared at him and leapt back. The young cat stopped instantly, sat back, and licked his fur into place.

Wise Teacher waited patiently for him to finish, watching the crest of the bank. Then he went quickly up the little ravine the runoff had cut in the bank, crouching just before it opened out onto the top of the bank and the street. He poked his head up and took a quick look, pulled it back, and then took a second, longer look.

He looked back over his shoulder. Water Walker had already begun his climb. He came immediately up behind Wise Teacher and crouched. Wise Teacher poked his head up again and checked for dogs, people, cars, and the thousand other dangers a running cat has trouble keeping track of. When he was sure it was clear, he bolted up out of the ditch and across the street. When he looked back, Water Walker was not at his heels.

He walked back to the curb and looked back across the street. The delicate head poked up out of the narrow ravine, looked right and left and disappeared. In a moment, the youngster poked his head up again, checked once, and shot across the street. Wise Teacher turned to the sidewalk without comment. He trotted toward the lot and the hub of his late afternoon rounds. He could hear the soft, wet footsteps of Water Walker right behind him. With a few months' training, a cat who picked up things that fast might allow a wise teacher to save enough energy to live forever.

When he felt Water Walker begin to go by him, he was not sure. He wondered if it was not Carrunner all over again. When they went by the front of the house, it was almost a footrace, and Wise Teacher had a quizzical look on his face that was somewhere between exasperation and joy. Water Walker moved almost even with him, intent, watching his every move the way Carrunner used to, and when I saw them moving like that, I wondered if maybe there wasn't something to reincarnation after all.